D1035834

THE SOUL OF THE NATIONS

THE SOUL OF THE NATIONS

Addresses delivered at the

INTERNATIONAL CONGRESS OF UNIVERSAL CHRISTIAN HUMANISM

THE BRUSSELS WORLD EXHIBITION, MAY, 1958

THE BRUCE PUBLISHING COMPANY • MILWAUKEE

NIHIL OBSTAT:

John F. Murphy, S.T.D.
Censor librorum

IMPRIMATUR:

✠ William E. Cousins
Archbishop of Milwaukee

March 12, 1960

Library of Congress Catalog Card Number: 60–11981

CONTENTS

THE SOUL OF THE NATIONS

THE SOUL OF THE NATIONS

INTRODUCTION

BY FATHER GABRIEL BOUTSEN, O.F.M. . . . *Born, Belgium, September 23, 1903; entered the Order of St. Francis, 1920; ordained, 1928; China missionary, 1929–1945; chaplain "Flying Tigers, U. S. A.," 1944–1945; lectured through Belgium, Holland, and the U.S.A.; traveled extensively in Europe, Asia, Africa, Australia, America; speaker on "The Te Deum Conference," 1958–1959; writer of many books; secretary of the First World Congress of Universal Christian Humanism (Brussels World Fair, 1958); Cultural Attaché in the Vatican pavilion at the same exhibit*

For the first time in history, a universal and international exhibition was built on ideological ground, at Brussels in 1958. Therefore, and for the first time, the Vatican erected its own pavilion and ordered the Fathers Superior of Missionary Orders in Belgium to organize a world Congress of "Universal Christian Humanism" within the general framework of the Brussels 58 U.I.E. and the particular one of *Civitas Dei*.

The theme to be chosen would be THE SOUL OF THE NATIONS, and by nations was meant the big ethnologic groups of people, including practically the whole of mankind: China, Japan, India, the Middle East, Europe, Africa, North and South America. What was meant by THE SOUL OF THE NATIONS was clearly explained by the leitmotiv of the exhibition, i.e., to display "spiritual values for a better world."

An appeal was made to fifty-two nations, who forwarded their best products to Brussels, everything they could show in the artistic and technical spheres. They contributed something spiritual, too, in the way of sacrifices, since, in spite of the hostility existing in the actual relations between some countries, they had to keep quite close to each other and bear differences patiently for six months! For the first time in human history, this old prophecy was realized: "And I saw the lion resting closely near the calf, and the leopard at the side of the sheep."

Nevertheless, little was said about the superior part of man. All these pavilions could not display more than "they had." We needed a Congress where people could show and say who and what they were.

Our Congress was placed on a very high level. It did not concern itself with all the values of a whole people, but with the personal value, the spirit, the being, the soul of each. So we reduced the world into nine important units and we appealed to the most representative scholars of all countries. We would invite them all to Brussels and we would build with these nine "sages" a kind of spiritual atomium that would attract the attention of millions of people otherwise so much distracted by the many pavilions of the exhibition.

The Congress would take place on Whitsun week, Tuesday the twenty-seventh and Wednesday the twenty-eighth of May, 1958. We would bring with us the Holy Ghost Himself.

Our object was to organize a World-Pentecost Festival between people who mustered in force and were no longer Parthians and Medes, Cretes and Arabians, but Japanese and Chinese, Indians and Arabians, Africans and Europeans, and the inhabitants of the New World, North and South America. The countries that had no pavilion at the exhibition, such as India and Chile, among others, were included in the Pentecost Concert organized by our Congress.

The significance of Pentecost was discussed by a distinguished theologian, His Excellency Msgr. L. Suenens, Auxiliary Bishop of Malines and representative of his Eminence Joseph Ernest Cardinal Van Roey, Primate of Belgium.

The object of the Congress was "the Soul of the Nations." It was essentially therefore a psychoanalysis of the human being, but acknowledging that the Divine Spirit enlightens the higher and immaterial part of the individual and collective soul, just as the sun enlightens the top of the mountains emerging above the clouds.

The Congress was a big success, because the subject was treated by eminent psychologists and theologians.

Who were these masters?

For China, Professor John C. H. Wu, of Seton Hall University, Newark, N. J., U. S. A.

For Japan, Professor Joseph Yokira, of the University of Kobe (Economics).

For India, Reverend F. Jerome D'Souza, councilor at the United Nations.

For the Middle East, Monsignor Filip Nabaa, Archbishop of Beirouth.

For Europe, Professor H. Brugmans, rector of the European College at Bruges.

For Africa, Reverend Joseph Malula, parish priest at Leopoldville.

For North America, Monsignor Vincent Jeffers, representative of His Eminence Francis Joseph Cardinal Spellman of the United States.

For South America, Sir James Bruron Subiabre of Santiago, Chile.

And for Russia, Professor Irene Posnoff, head of the Russian section at the Vatican pavilion.

When we asked the speakers to treat this entirely new subject, THE SOUL OF THE NATIONS, we did not refer to an independent collective soul, but to the most intimate spiritual reactions of a whole people in relation to Divinity, Man, Nature, Happiness, Life, Eternity, Christ, the Gospel, and the Church.

We wanted to determine on a world scale: Why do people live? Why and for whose sake are they prepared to die? Why do they laugh? Why do they weep? What do they consider worth working for? What is their idea of happiness or misfortune?

By reason of their ethnological and cultural unity and uniformity the answers would be quite simple for countries like China and Japan. But think of the difficulties to overcome and the great effort to be exerted to interpret the soul of nations such as India, the Middle East, Europe, and South America. On what basis could a lecture concerning the unity and the soul of these countries be developed?

To get a genuine and complete picture we asked the speakers to keep in touch during a period of two years with other scholars in their various countries. Eight Committees were established this way in various parts of the world to study the soul of their own nation.

The Apostolic Nuncios in Tokyo and in South America, together with His Eminence Cardinal Gracias of Bombay, His Excellency Msgr. Thomas Potacamur of Bangalore, secretary to the National Conference of Bishops for the whole of India, who on the occasion of a plenary sitting delegated the Rev. F. Jerome D'Souza, and His Excellency Msgr. Scalais of Leopoldville took an active part in the preparation.

The Congress was presided over by His Excellency Msgr. Van Wayenbergh, Rector Magnificus of the University of Louvain. His assistants were Doctor De Raeymaeker and Doctor Draeye. The Reverend F. A. Lievens, councilor at the Vatican pavilion, saw to the inclusion of the Congress in the general framework of *Civitas Dei.*

The speakers were introduced by Minister of State A. E. De Schryver, toastmaster. The texts of the lectures were obviously not censured. We left the speakers full responsibility for their lecture, its form as well as content.

The Congress was most successful. It brought to light the greatest treasures of all men, revealed the secret of various cultural, religious, and technical marvels, and afforded opportunity to visit the respective pavilions in a practical way.

All the lecturers found it necessary to point out a definite dualism among their own people. They argued that a person abandoned to himself cannot get well and be cured of his deficiencies; he finds a reason therefore to seek his salvation in the Gospel and a means to sanity even in this world. Atheist humanism had to be discarded for experimental reasons. All agreed that Christianity fully recognizes individual and national rights.

It is of course possible to speak about God to Japanese, Bantoes, Chinese, etc.; but according to the conclusions to be drawn from the following reports, we must remember that, though it is the same God we are speaking of to various people, we cannot always speak of Him in the same way. This is a principle of value to all missionaries, as well as to others who by reason of their professional or other duties are in contact with people living in other parts of the world. So far there has been too much sameness in the presentation of Christian thought to all the nations. Uniformity if useful and necessary, but nevertheless the diversity of the various peoples must also be respected. This policy will be found advisable and indispensable for the propagation of the Faith.

The lectures could not, of course, be presented in Western fashion. Rich diversity in literary style, form, and diction belongs to THE SOUL OF THE NATIONS. Nevertheless, we beg to introduce them here in their entirety. This collection constitutes a unique book. It is the story of the world contained in a "pocket edition," but it is the story of the "whole" world. It is a picture of the world's Soul.

In this short description of the First World Congress of Universal Christian Humanism, we bear witness that it was the result of a tremendous intellectual work that lasted several years. This effort expended on a world-wide scale has made us the possessors of uncounted, undisclosed, and almost unknown views and facts. When it is so difficult in these "encyclopedic" days to tell anything new, how amazing it is to be confronted here by a world almost completely ignored until now. It is no less astonishing to find that the world could remain so good, when on the one hand it may dispose of so many sources of energy, and on the other hand be ignorant of so many cravings concealed in the soul of the world and revealed for the first time by this Congress.

This edition was made possible through the kind assistance of Dr. John Donovan and the Rev. F. Adhemar De Pauw, O.F.M. The Congress and the editor thank them most sincerely.

THE MYSTERY OF PENTECOST STILL CONTINUES

BY **BISHOP LEO-JOSEPH SUENENS** . . . *Born, Brussels, 1912; first Auxiliary Bishop of Malines; author of* The Theology Of The Apostolate, The Gospel To Every Creature, Life of Edel Quinn; *representative of His Eminence Ernest Joseph Cardinal Van Roey, at the World Congress of Universal Christian Humanism*

The present Congress is held under the sign of Pentecost. This is more than a happy coincidence, because Pentecost is the festival day of the world expansion of the Church, of her catholicity and universality. The catholicity of the Church appears openly on the very morning of Pentecost. "We all, Parthians, and Medes, and Elamites, and inhabitants of Mesopotamia, Judea and Cappadocia, Pontus and Asia, Phrygia and Pamphylia, Egypt and the parts of Libya about Cyrene, and strangers of Rome, Cretes and Arabians, we have heard them speak in our own tongues the wonderful works of God." So relate the Acts of the Apostles: the expansion of the Church as well as her universal adaptation is already in the bud in this very early account.

The presence here of Christians coming from all countries of the world, from Asia as from Africa, from the Old as well as from the New World, bears witness that the Church never ceases to announce to everybody, "in his own tongue, the wonderful works of God."

On the occasion of this brotherly meeting, it may be good to refer to this first morning of the Church, to contemplate more closely what occurred in the upper room, to make again this pilgrimage to the sources.

If we want to grasp the ultimate reason for the enormous apostolic effort expended by the Church, we must return often to this statement, placed at the center of our Credo: *Et incarnatus est de Spiritu Sancto ex Maria Virgine.* Christ was born by the operation of the Holy Ghost, thanks to the co-operation of Mary.

Christianity may be defined as "an exchange of two loves in Jesus Christ." The personal and lively Love that comes down from heaven to effect the sacred alliance and brings with it the gift of the Father and of the Son is called the Holy Ghost. The human love that rises from the earth to meet Him and is supported by a superior grace is called Mary. These two loves are infinitely distant from each other, as the uncreated is from the created. But they converge, by the will of God, toward Jesus Christ, placed at the crossing point of this encounter, and born from this mysterious alliance between the Holy Ghost and Mary.

What occurred historically in the visible birth of Jesus continues in the invisible birth of Christ in the souls of men, in the birth of the Mystical Body. And the apostolate is nothing else than the work undertaken to cause Christ to be born or to grow in men's souls.

To reach the core of any sound apostolate, we must be conscious of the encounter between the Holy Ghost and Mary; we must translate in the detail of any apostolic gesture, the central statement of our Credo, and our apostolate must be accomplished "in Spiritu Sancto, ex Maria Virgine."

We would like, because our time is limited, to stress more especially here the "spiritual" aspect of the Catholic apostolate, and for this reason this lecture is entitled "The Mystery of Pentecost Still Continues." But we shall not forget that the Queen of the Apostles presided at the Cenacle during this outpouring of the Holy Spirit.

To grasp the continuity of the Christian apostolate, it is important to understand this statement of St. Paul, that the gifts of God are without repentance. Inherent in all the designs of God there is consistency and continuity. Time does no more than unfold and bring to light what is implicit in His unique concept, which is from eternity. God does not go about His work unsystematically. He does not touch up or go back over what He has done. Still less does He suddenly alter His plans or procedures. God knows nothing of experimentation or broken alliances. We have in heaven a "faithful witness." His ways, unsearchable, diverse, frequently baffling though they may be, preserve nonetheless their unity and constancy of purpose. In the light of this law of divine action it is easier to understand that the events reported in the Gospel are not stories without sequel; they are not unrelated happenings that died with the hour. Beyond the events that took place in the setting of Palestine, and were colored by their setting, faith reveals to us a mystery, valid for every age. He who is Eternal is there, introduced into time. He who is Unchanging makes Himself known in passing events. He who is Absolute speaks of Himself through what is relative and contingent in a local situation or in a chance meeting. What else is the mystery of the Incarnation but the coming of God into space and time, God becoming man so as to reveal to the world, in images, in parables taken from life, what the eye has not seen, nor the ear heard, what has not entered into the heart or mind of man? The Word of God is uttered in time, but transcends time. The Word is made flesh, but does not renounce its divine origin. Henceforward we come to know God by seeing Him living among us and we learn our incomparable lesson intuitively, merely by studying facts. Our metaphysic is personified, brought before our eyes as though on film.

The mystery of the Upper Room, when contemplated at this level of faith, is an expression of the law of the apostolate, valid for all time.

The Master had said: "You shall receive the power of the Holy Ghost coming upon you, and you shall be witnesses unto me in Jerusalem, and in all Judea and Samaria, and even to the uttermost parts of the earth." This promise is not directed only to the Twelve. Henceforth, in order to give testimony to Christ, men must have received the Holy Spirit, be clothed in His strength, covered over by His shadow. An apostle of Christ who has not received this baptism of water and fire, who has not duly put on the Spirit of God, is unthinkable. This is required not only if he is to be equipped for the ministry of the pulpit, but even if he is to fulfill more modest tasks of a profane and temporal nature.

The account in Acts of the election of the seven deacons comes to mind; it is as rich in suggestion as one could wish for. "The number of disciples increasing," St. Luke tells us, "there arose a murmuring of the Greeks against the Hebrews, for that their widows were neglected in the daily ministration." Here there is a conflict of interests, a matter of the sharing-out of assistance. A more down-to-earth or more prosaic problem than this one of social justice could not be thought of. A solution could be found, one would think, with just a minimum of common sense, tact, and simple arithmetic. How are the Apostles going to deal with this ticklish question which is thrust upon them? The attitude they adopt will serve to indicate to us their practical understanding of the mystery of God. They called together all their disciples and said to them: "It is not reason that we should leave the word of God and serve tables. Wherefore, brethren, look ye out among you seven men of good reputation, full of the Holy Ghost and wisdom, whom we may appoint over this business." Let us examine these words. What criterion determines their choice? What are they looking for primarily? Men filled with the Spirit. In their eyes this fullness of the Spirit is an indispensable condition for the success of this humble, daily task. Dependence on the Holy Spirit is the key to success of such a mission. The Holy Spirit must find adaptable and obedient instruments in His hands if the service of tables is to achieve its full purpose. It was precisely in this fashion that the early disciples understood things. "And the saying was liked by all the multitude," says St. Luke. "And they chose Stephen, a man full of faith and of the Holy Ghost, and Philip, and Prochorus, and Nicanor, and Timon, and Parmenas, and Nicolas a proselyte of Antioch."

This has even greater validity when it comes to less mundane tasks. From this time forward, whenever the Church has important duties to entrust to her children, she begs for them an increased outpouring of the Holy Spirit: "Receive ye the Holy Spirit," says the bishop to those he is about to ordain deacons, "that He may be your strength in resisting the devil and his temptations."

"Receive ye the Holy Spirit," he says again to the priests who are about to receive from him the power of absolution. "Whose sins you shall forgive, they are forgiven them; whose sins you shall retain, they are retained." And when the consecrator imposes his hands in the consecration of a new bishop, he says to him simply: "Receive the Holy Spirit"; thus marking him forever for his high mission. Such is the practice of the Church which takes its origin from the mystery of Pentecost.

If we are to grasp the continuity of the plan of God and penetrate the hidden soul of the Church, we must constantly return to the consideration of what happened in the Upper Room. An apostolate divorced from the Holy Spirit is doomed to sterility: it has lost its soul. Let us spend some time, then, in considering that Upper Room in Jerusalem, from which the Church came forth, and where the Christian apostolate was born. This retreat ordered by Christ at His Ascension is the prototype of every true and fruitful retreat. There is to be found here that indissoluble union of prayer and action which is always the framework of the visible development of the Church.

The Upper Room: a place of silence where words are put aside so that God may speak, where the soul opens itself gently to the assault of grace, where recollection calls on, and prepares the way for, the great wind that is to blow round the house.

The Upper Room: a place from which men set out to conquer the world. "Home is where one starts from," wrote Eliot.

When the Spirit of God has come down and has fulfilled His mission of transfiguration, the invitation is to go out from the Upper Room. Do not the symbols themselves contain an undeniable call to the crusade of the apostolate? The Holy Spirit no longer appears in the form of a dove, but as parted tongues of fire which rested on each of the Apostles. Nothing happens by chance so far as God is concerned and this very symbolism cloaks a command. Tongues: symbol and instrument of speech. It is a call to go out to men and to announce to them in a firm voice the Gospel of God. The spoken word takes precedence over the written word. Living tradition had a start on the interpretation of texts which at the first Pentecost had not yet been written and which were destined to be nothing more than the faithful reflection of the Apostles' preaching. Even if an atom bomb were tomorrow to destroy all the books in the world, the Church would be unaffected essentially as long as the living word of God is free to spread itself abroad.

Faith comes from hearing — faith is passed on by word of mouth from man to man. There is an obligation on us to speak to our brethren and tell them the marvelous story of a God who loves us with a love that overcomes all obstacles. There is an obligation on us to announce to them the good news. The Gospel cannot be brought to the hearing of all men if Christians do not speak of it and proclaim their faith.

If the symbol of tongues expresses an invitation to preach the Gospel, that of fire bears a like call to communication. Nothing spreads like fire. The Master has said: "I am come to bring fire upon the earth, and what will I but that it be lighted?" We have no right to smother this fire, no right to bury it with ashes. Every Christian ought to be a torch, able to "set light to a whole procession" at his contact. *Cursores hominum lampada tradunt.* This sacred fire must be handed on to the generations to come. This fire is the Spirit of Pentecost, the soul of the Church, for the Holy Spirit is the strength of her word, the breathing of her soul, and the joy of her heart.

Going to the heart of the mystery of the Upper Room, we shall understand better the urgent necessity of animating our apostolate with the breath of the Spirit. This meditation will help us to realize that our activities have meaning and bear fruit only in the measure that Another than us acts and speaks by our mouths. For we must love men with the Love of God Himself, with the living and personal Love that is the Holy Spirit, supreme Prophet and Gift of the other two divine Persons. This is the starting point of all supernatural action. Here we must ceaselessly return, under pain of straying from the way. It is not we ourselves who go to seek after souls, but God in us. He takes the initiative; He loves the first. *Ipse prior dilexit nos.* We have to enter into this Love of God which goes before our own, and allow ourselves to be transformed by it. It is not enough to love men *for* the love of God with our own poor love. We have to love them *with* the magnanimous, implacable love of God Himself. Held captive by His grace, our heart will be armed to face the inevitable checks, ingratitude, bruises. Is not the Love of God sheltered from these changes of fortune, from this rise and fall of the tide? Is it not unadulterated, giving, fidelity, liberality? The love of God does not depend on our co-operation. A love for men which finds its source in Him is like to God Himself, firm as a rock and unshakeable. If it is our desire to carry through our apostolic tasks in spite of the ruggedness of the way we have no alternative but to love men *in Spiritu Sancto* or else to renounce an undertaking beyond our powers. It is well to face squarely this decisive choice and to realize its consequences. To leave an entry into oneself for the Holy Spirit so that He may accomplish His mission through us: that is the basic duty of the apostle, that is, of every one who has been baptized.

We should add that in order to wait for the Spirit with open heart and to offer Him a pliant spirit, we must unite ourselves closely to her who received the Holy Spirit in an unparalleled fullness. It is not by chance that the Blessed Virgin is there in the Upper Room preparing the disciples for the coming of the Paraclete. Her office as Mediatrix of all graces calls for her to be present where the outpouring of the Spirit marks the visible inauguration of the Kingdom of her Son on earth. This presence, or rather this union with Mary, is also a law of supernatural life. Jesus is born of the Holy Spirit and Mary. It is fitting that the mystical Christ be born and come to maturity in souls in like fashion. Pentecost is the continuation of the Incarnation; the Virgin of Bethlehem will be also the Queen of the Cenacle. If the Church is "Jesus Christ shared and spread abroad," the Mother of Jesus must be the Mother of the Church. Her presence in the Upper Room is an indication for all future ages that wherever the Holy Spirit gives Himself, Mary is at hand to prepare souls to welcome Him. Her mediation is always at work in the hidden places of souls, even if we are unaware of it. "And the mother of Jesus was there"; this is a law of history. It tells us that Mary is always where the mystery of Pentecost is being continued.

And so today the Church invites all men to go back to the pure sources of her apostolic spirit, and to take a better measure of the task to be accomplished. The Cenacle is the cradle of the Church, her Epiphany. It is also the starting point for the enormous impetus which brings the Church toward a world that starves because it ignores the message of Christ. "Is there a greater peril for the world than not to open itself to Christ?" asked St. Hilary. The missionary impetus is eminently an impulse of civilization and humanism. Considering that the theme of the Exhibition invites us to point out the contribution of Christianity and religion toward the happiness of man, we may be satisfied to say that the superior part of our civilization is the expression and the translation into life of the message brought all over the world by the successors of the Apostles, by those who transmitted the fire of Pentecost from past ages to ages yet unborn.

We must endeavor to concentrate all our physical and supernatural efforts that the present ages may be enlightened by the light and warmed by the heat of that fire.

Christianity as an instrument of personal and social happiness must necessarily be provided with life-giving sap, and it should be a Christianity absolutely integral in all respects.

Some have wanted to break away and humanize the world, make it more inhabitable, improve all of life's conditions *before* bringing in the Gospel at all. We reject this dissociation which would put the Gospel to rest until the world is ready to accept it.

In a sense, the world will never be ready, because the Gospel is such disturbing and unexpected news that it will always outrun and bewilder the most daring expectations of men.

The world was not ready to hear its Master: a glance at Calvary furnishes enough evidence of this.

The world was not ready to listen to the Apostles: suffice it to read over the pages of the Acts depicting St. Paul at the Agora in Athens.

The world is not ready now to speak for itself: just listen to the noise it makes in an effort to forget its troubles, and observe by what variety of means it causes itself to be "distracted" from God.

But there is danger in inviting God's messengers to keep silent even for a moment. Even now, the world may be ready to listen to us, but the truth is we are not ready to speak to the world. *Credidi propter quod locutus sum.*

The tongues of fire on Pentecost remain an important symbol. We must go to the world with the Gospel, but with a Gospel that impregnates the whole of individual, social, economical, national, and international life. The world can be humanized by being evangelized or, vice versa, it can be evangelized while being humanized. Let the mystery of Pentecost reach its full dimensions and the spirit will glide over the renovated world as it glided in the beginning over the whole creation that came out of the hands of God. *Emitte Spiritum tuum et creabuntur et renovabis faciem terrae.*

NORTH AMERICA

BY MSGR. VINCENT W. JEFFERS . . . *Born, July 19, 1907, in Tucahoe, New York.* EDUCATION: *Our Lady of Lourdes Elementary School; Regis High School (Jesuit Fathers); St. John's College, Fordham University; Fordham Graduate School of Philosophy; St. Joseph's Seminary, Dunwoodie, Yonkers, New York. Ordained, December 19, 1931.* APPOINTMENTS: *The Society for the Propagation of the Faith, in 1934; Archdiocesan Director, 1949; Papal Chamberlain to Pope Pius XII, 1950; Domestic Prelate, 1957.* TRAVELS: *Missions in U. S., Canada, Mexico, South America, Caribbean Islands, Hawaii, Guam, Africa (particularly Ruanda Urundi, Belgian Congo), and Europe*

For centuries man has noted important events by the ringing of bells. On July 4, 1776, in the city of Philadelphia, the now revered Liberty Bell sounded the birth of a nation, dedicated to the proposition that all men are equal and free. The Declaration of Independence expresses basic religious Christian principles: "We hold these truths to be self-evident that all men are created equal, that all are endowed by their Creator with certain unalienable Rights, that among these are Life, Liberty and the Pursuit of Happiness."

There is a striking similarity of thought and language between the text of the Declaration of Independence and the writings of eminent theologians. On such topics as the Equality of Man, the Function of Government, the Source of Power, and the Right to Change Government the author of the Declaration of Independence seems to agree with St. Thomas Aquinas and St. Robert Bellarmine.

For the practical operation of the principles contained in the

Declaration of Independence, the new nation adopted a Constitution. The First Amendment reads: "Congress shall make no law respecting an establishment of religion or prohibiting the free exercise thereof —" It is evident that here is allowed freedom of religion. Congress may not establish an official religion nor may Congress restrict the free exercise of religion. As Pope Leo XIII said in his encyclical letter to the American hierarchy on January 6, 1895: "For the Church amongst you, fettered by no hostile legislation, protected against violence by the common laws and the impartiality of the tribunals, is free to live and act without hindrance."

The American tradition, however, goes far beyond a mere grant of religious freedom. Ever since the beginning of the nation, the federal government and the various state governments have actively co-operated with religion and have often supported religion in general without showing favoritism to any one particular denomination. The federal government, for instance, has paid the salaries of chaplains in the military service, has provided free lunches for Catholic as well as public school children, and has paid tuition for former soldiers and sailors to become priests, ministers, or rabbis. State governments have zoning laws to protect churches and schools.

Traditionally, therefore, Church-State separation in America has not meant that the government is hostile to the Church nor has it barred aid to religion in general. At the present time, certain groups in the United States construe the ban on an established church to mean a prohibition of any aid from government to religion. If this interpretation should be sustained by the courts in the future, it would constitute a radical departure from ages-old American tradition.

Because religion is so closely interwoven into American history and culture, it can truly be said that the American way of life is basically a religious way of life. In the Zorach vs. Clauson case, the Supreme Court of the United States said very aptly: "We are a religious people whose institutions presuppose a Supreme Being." The Founding Fathers of America were religious men and it is still customary to open sessions of Congress with prayer. On American coins can be found the motto: "In God We Trust." In the pledge of allegiance to the American flag, the citizen pledges loyalty to "one nation under God, indivisible, with liberty and justice for all." As President Eisenhower said when he signed the act that added *under God* to the pledge: ". . . in this way we are reaffirming the transcendence of religious faith in America's heritage and future; in this way we shall constantly strengthen those spiritual weapons which forever will be our country's most powerful resource in peace and war."

Now I would not want to give the impression that America is a thoroughly Christian nation, professing belief in the fundamentals of the faith given to the Apostles. The people are fundamentally religious but their expression of faith has often taken exotic and eccentric forms. The Protestants, for instance, lacking the unifying force of Church authority, have tended to break out into an exuberant profusion of diverse and contradictory sects. There are at least 250 different Protestant denominations in the country and new groups are constantly appearing. Then of course there are at least six million Jews in the United States and millions of secularists who have only slight leanings toward religion.

At the present time, there are more church members than ever before in American history. Eighty-two per cent of the people are affiliated with some denomination. This means little in some cases. Certain church members almost never attend the church of their choice. Yet at the same time it can be said that religion is more popular in America today than at any time in the past 150 years.

Some call this vast renewal of religious interest a religious revival. However, there are certain aspects of the trend that are questionable, and for that reason I would not want to describe this increase of interest in religion as a genuine religious revival. Some foreign commentators have called it a spiritual renascence and a Catholic editor in South Africa called it "The New American Revolution." It may be a revolution, a turning away from the left-wing radicalism so prevalent twenty years ago in America, but that does not make it a true revival.

What are the evidences of this new stirring of interest in religion in America? They are countless. Many religious novels are best sellers and there has been a marked increase in recent years in the sale of all kinds of religious literature; religious movies are good box-office attractions; vague religious songs are very popular; cards giving the words of "Grace" before and after meals are to be found in the dining cars of many trains; business executives often open their meetings with prayer; and this is true also of meetings of the President's Cabinet. President Eisenhower himself has enrolled as a Presbyterian. In short, religion is "popular" in America today and very few are the Americans who will admit they are atheists or agnostics.

The causes of this renewal of interest are many. There is the threat of the H-bomb, for instance, which impels some men and women to look for religion as a means of inner security. There is also the menace of atheistic Communism. Many Americans feel that we have to be strong to cope with Communism and therefore there is need for America to return to religious faith, which they rightly feel was the source of America's strength in its beginnings.

Whatever the cause, the fact is that religion is enjoying great prestige today. Yet I alleged that this did not amount to a religious revival. Why? Because I feel that the religion that is generally found outside Catholic circles in America is often a vague faith in faith. It is a wishful, optimistic hope that problems will disappear. It fixes its attention on the removing of the problems rather than on the worship of God. That is, religion is looked to as something that will produce material or psychological results. Some Americans want to cultivate religion as a means of preserving national security. Others want to use religion as a means of acquiring peace of mind. In other words, they are using religion as a means to an end not as an end in itself. Religion, which is transcendent as a goal (the final goal of our striving), thus becomes a means to a worldly end. This betrays a grave distortion of values. Religion cannot be reduced to the status of a means to some material or physical end. "Seek first the kingdom of God and his justice and all things shall be given you besides" (Mt. 6:33). But some Americans are seeking these other things primarily rather than the Kingdom of God and His justice.

This is not true of American Catholics and of certain other groups of orthodox believers. But I would say that the "popular" trend in religion in America is to use religion for worldly ends. This probably derives from the fact that so many popular leaders talk vaguely about religion as a sort of faith in faith and the general public takes this to mean a feeling of assurance that all will be well in the immediate future.

At the same time, it cannot be denied that the fact that religion is "popular" is a step forward. It marks at least a pause in the progress of secularism and a distinct break with the doctrinaire materialism so popular twenty years ago. It turns its back on atheism and looks to religion with a healthy respect and admiration.

This renunciation of materialism appears especially in American education. No sectarian teaching is allowed in the public schools but there is a growing demand for programs to inculcate moral and spiritual values in the classroom. This demand derives not only from parents but from teachers as well. It is not easy for all religions to agree on a set of fundamental moral and spiritual values that they hold in common. Yet in New York City, for instance, the Board of Education has inaugurated such a program with the approval of the major faiths. Moreover, the Supreme Court in the Zorach *vs.* Clauson case upheld a New York statute providing for a program of religious instruction for public school children during public school hours but off the premises of the public school building. The Court said: "We find no Constitutional requirement which makes it necessary for government to be hostile to religion and to throw its weight against efforts to widen the effective scope of religious influence." By adjusting the public school schedule to off-premises religious instruction the State, according to the Court, "respects the religious nature of our people and accommodates the public service to their spiritual needs."

At college level, courses in religion are given by representatives of the various faiths at many privately owned institutions. In tax-supported state universities, educators may not impart sectarian instruction on the premises. Yet a movement is under way to teach religion at these publicly owned institutions not as religion but as a feature of American history and culture. Many professors find, for instance, that students cannot understand the classics of our literature unless they are acquainted with the doctrines of sin, redemption and grace, and the biblical personalities that figure so prominently in American literature courses.

More encouraging than the religious effervescence at the popular level is this notable stirring of the spirit among the better-educated. In his recent *Reflections on America*, Jacques Maritain points to the prevalent concern among American educators for "moral and spiritual value programs." He notes also as a sign of spiritual renewal the trend to the contemplative life found among American Catholics. The one monastery at Gethsemani, Kentucky, according to Maritain, has more novices than can be found in all European Trappist monasteries combined.

American Protestantism long ago ceased to be a theological Protestantism. Outside of Catholic circles, the American believer has generally tended to look on religion not as a matter of creed but of personal religious experience and of service to neighbor. Today, however, there is at least the beginning of a definite return to theology among Protestant thinkers. At the Faith and Order Conference of the World Council of Churches (for North America) at Oberlin, Ohio, September, 1957, many delegates noticed a pronounced and aggressive movement to bring Protestantism back to theological foundations. The theologians at Oberlin were convinced that any hope for Christian reunion lies not in mere good fellowship but in a sincere attempt to examine the question of unity in the light of the Gospel.

The religious experience which Americans cherish is generally an experience of God present in nature, in the woods and seashore, in the rolling plains and starry skies. Every year the President of the United States issues a Thanksgiving Proclamation asking all Americans to give thanks to God for His natural bounty. Probably because so much of American history has been frontier history,

Americans are lovers of "the great outdoors." Many claim to experience an awareness of God's presence much more readily in the beauties of nature than in the solemnity of a religious service in church.

However, I do believe that Protestants usually think of religion as a service to neighbor rather than an inner experience. They show a real concern for the whole local community and they expect a Christian to be first and foremost a good citizen.

This may appear to foreigners as an adulteration of religion to mere social service. But anyone who has lived long in America sees it as more than that. This willingness to serve is but an outward expression of the basic Christian precept to love one another while the desire for good citizenship is the practice of the virtue of piety. The background of America is European; a spark of the Gospel teaching lies deep in the people, even in those who do not speak the Gospel.

It is said that in the hierarchy of values, goodness rates first in America. I think it is true that Americans do prize goodness over intelligence. Human reliability, devotion, and helpfulness are the top values in America. This esteem for sociability often creates difficulties for the Catholic. For he holds to the ability of the mind to attain to truth, natural or revealed; while some Americans feel that anyone who holds doggedly to a doctrine is intolerant.

It is laboring the obvious to say that Americans use the latest technological devices. But they do not regard them as sacred or allow them to depersonalize their lives. Of course, there are exceptions. Here and there you will find factories where assembly-line work tends to make robots out of workers. But management and organized labor have co-operated earnestly in most cases to improve working conditions as much as possible. The great labor unions have been adamant in their demands that the worker be respected as a human being and management has found that it is "enlightened self-interest" to improve conditions. Satisfied workers are better workers. Happiness increases efficiency.

This brings me to the charge that American capitalism is an evil force. *Laissez-faire* capitalism was imported from Europe. It was alien to the American spirit of freedom. Over the years the American people have been striving to free themselves from this structure for their idealism and generosity run counter to the brutal ruthlessness of old-fashioned capitalism.

The result is that today in America the industrial system is no longer a system of cutthroat, dog-eat-dog competition. Management and labor are trying sincerely to work together to bring about a system that recognizes the worker as a person. I think it would surprise some non-Americans to see hundreds of business executives and laboring men having breakfast together. This happens frequently in our big cities when industries hold Communion breakfasts at big hotels. All receive Communion at Mass and then go to the hotel for breakfast.

It is evident that American industry has passed beyond the old capitalism and inaugurated a radically new system of labor-management relations. Legislation enacted by the federal and state government on this all-important matter reveals an effort to realize in practice many principles enumerated in the encyclicals of Leo XIII and Pius XI. The American system is not perfect. Many are its flaws; but it is a step in the direction of the Christian ideal of the inherent dignity of the workingman. Unfortunately, America has not publicized this fact sufficiently to the world, and so the peoples in Asia, for instance, think of America as a "capitalist" country, in the bad sense of that word. Why this failure on the part of America to tell the world about the change? Perhaps it is due to American indifference to philosophy. The Americans are content to produce a good system that operates successfully. They are too pragmatic to formulate the philosophy behind the system and to communicate it to the world. They are satisfied to see a project or a system work. They are interested in technology not in ideology.

Are Americans materialistic? Do they love dollars more than the things of the spirit? It is true that Americans are not ashamed to talk about money but they are ashamed of avarice. Americans get money, not to hoard it, but to use it for laudable purposes. Witness the astounding gifts to charities! Witness also the work of the great foundations which give money for civic, educational, and charitable projects! The spiritual person is not one who has an aristocratic contempt for social improvement. He is rather the man who uses money *generously* to help the poor and to raise the general level of living.

Of many charities mention is made of two: the missions and the needy of the world. America, child of European generosity, has grown to become the strong support of the Pontifical Mission Works and individual mission needs.

Blessed by God with abundance, America has been led by a Christlike hierarchy through its own Catholic Relief Services to understand by action true devotion to the poor. A constant flow of food, medicine, clothing to the needy bespeaks a love of God, animated by good deeds. Foremost in this offshore charity of the American Church is His Eminence, Francis Cardinal Spellman, whom I represent here today. As Military Vicar he visits troops in every part of the world. On his way to and fro he spends time with missionaries, encouraging and aiding them. On his visits to the refugees he embodies American good will and generosity.

Lest I give the impression that the American people are angelic, I must point out some of the dark spots on the American scene. In the first place, the American public, as I have mentioned before, is anti-intellectual. It does not accord any great prestige to thinkers and tends sometimes to look upon them with suspicion. It calls them "eggheads," meaning persons whose thinking is so unrealistic that they are easy dupes for Communist agitators.

A second dark spot in the American picture is the present obsession with sex. I suppose that this is a current phenomenon throughout the Western world in general, but it can be said that while this obsession is less depraved in the United States than in certain sophisticated circles in Europe, it is sillier than in Europe. It is silly because we have the spectacle of learned writers and professors *scientifically* expounding information that nature gives readily to the most uneducated. This sex obsession is not only objectionable for spiritual reasons but it also has a debilitating influence on mental health.

The third sordid feature of the American scene is racial discrimination. Fortunately, the Supreme Court has been bearing down heavily to invalidate laws in the Southern states that prescribe segregation of colored people from whites in schools, buses, trains, etc. The clergy, both Protestant and Catholic, have been active in creating a climate of opinion favorable to the Negro. It will take time to wipe out this legacy of evil but amazing progress has been made in the past few years.

It will be more difficult to eliminate racial discrimination in the North than segregation in the South. For this discrimination is not legal, but it can be practiced in subtle and devious ways. However, a very encouraging sign is the enactment in the Northern states of laws which forbid discrimination against Negroes in employment. Inevitably, discrimination and segregation must disappear for they are alien to the American spirit and there is a progressive awakening of public opinion against them.

Will America be converted? Let us look at the total picture. There is among Protestants and secularists a fear and distrust of the Church as an organized institution. This can be found in Liberal and Fundamentalist groups. In the early days of American history, Protestants opposed Catholicism for its religious doctrines. Later they disliked Catholics because they were immigrants who did not assimilate themselves to the American scene but lived in ghettos or colonies apart from the local native community. Today Catholics have become part of American social, industrial, and civic life.

The opposition to Catholicism now is a suspicion of the Church as a foreign organization, not a distrust of the members of the Church. Many non-Catholic agitators say they have no grievance against individual Catholics but they fear the hierarchy. When there is a discussion of the possibility of an American ambassador to the Vatican, immediately some Protestants see this as a move on the part of the hierarchy to get control of the American government. Some even go so far as to say that American Catholic bishops should be required to register as agents of a foreign power.

Certain Protestants feel strongly that the organized Catholic Church strikes too deeply into the personal liberties of Catholics and therefore it is a disturbing authoritarian force in a free, democratic society. What they reprobate most vigorously, however, is the work of Catholic organizations such as the Legion of Decency and the National Office for Decent Literature which indirectly affect non-Catholics. When the Legion or the NODL gives a bad rating to a movie or book, the managers of the movie houses and the sellers of the book necessarily suffer in their business. The Protestants claim that each Catholic should be allowed to decide for himself what movie he will attend or what book he will read — without advice from churchmen.

Again, enemies of the Church fear that the tolerance practiced by Catholics now is merely expedient. They claim that if Catholics become a majority of the voters in America, then the hierarchy will influence legislation to persecute Protestants.

On the other hand, the Protestants generally are ready and willing to express their admiration of the spiritual riches of the Catholic Church. They show a reverence for the Mass and the Sacraments, they manifest respect and admiration for the Catholic priests they happen to meet, they express sincere appreciation of the serenity and strength of Catholic faith and devotion. The increasing emphasis on liturgy in Protestant churches shows that they esteem Catholic ritual. They pay it the homage of imitation.

Last year more than 140,000 converts were received into the Catholic Church in the United States. That may seem a satisfying total but we must remember that there are 50,000 priests in the United States; as against the "leakage" from the Church, the convert total is not good.

Yet I am optimistic for the future. There are graphic indications that large numbers of Negroes will soon be asking for admission into the Church. Negro leaders have not been reticent in praising the Church for what it has done for them; and many Negroes, as they move to the North and to big cities away from the unlettered evangelism of the South, are looking for a more satisfying explanation of their relationship to God.

Moreover, I am supremely confident that in God's good time we will be able to demonstrate to our American non-Catholic friends that Catholicism is utterly congenial to the principles of the American

Republic. There are tensions between Catholics and Protestants due to the presence of a Church of authority in a democratic society. These tensions will disappear as a more apostolic and enlightened laity fill our American milieu with the rich fruits of Catholic culture in art, science, and literature as well as in the science of the saints.

America will not be converted tomorrow or the day after tomorrow, but there is a religious inspiration in the whole American way of life as well as a hunger for the spiritual. Let us conclude with a line from Maritain: "From this point of view, we may believe that if a new Christian civilization, a new Christendom, is ever to come about in human history, it is on American soil that it will find its starting point."

RUSSIA

BY **PROFESSOR IRENE POSNOFF** . . . *Born, Kiev (Russia), 1914; daughter of a famous Orthodox theologian; convert at Louvain University; devoted to the topics of Oriental Christianity; director of the Oriental Forum at Brussels; manager of two reviews:* Life With God *and* Russia and the Universal Church *(French); head of the Russian section at the Vatican pavilion*

The theme of the Russian soul has already been the object of numerous studies. I am afraid that by reason of the brevity of time presently afforded, I could not do much more than make a short synthesis of the salient points exposed by various thinkers. The general outlines of this presentation, unfortunately, cannot include many interesting and important details.

To understand the Russian soul, we must consider the influence exercised by Christianity. History throws a bright light on the close connections between religion and the Russian soul. It was after they had been baptized that our Russian forefathers began to acquire their national features and give witness to a cultural development. St. Olga and St. Vladimir are completely transformed after their conversion. We assist at the birth of a new man, regenerated in the waters of baptism.

From remote times, the paradox of Russian dualism is evident. Everywhere, but above all in Russia, "God and the Devil fight each other, and their battlefield is the heart of men" (Dostoevski); the light shineth in darkness, and the darkness did not comprehend it. Two different ways are clearly outlined through the whole of Russian history: the first one leads to the seeking of the truth, Christian justice, fidelity to the death for an ideal, humble love of

God and of neighbor, the building of the city of God in a sinful world; the other way is the proud struggle of fratricide, hatred, oppression of the weak, and complete atheism.

It is easier for a Russian to be good or bad than to be indifferent. Tendency toward the absolute in everything is the main feature of the Russian character. "As soon as our people reach the shore," so writes Dostoevski, "as soon as they think they have arrived there, they feel so happy that they go immediately to the extreme limits; what is the reason for it? . . . If one of us converts himself and becomes a Catholic, he also wants to become a Jesuit . . . if he becomes an atheist, he wants belief in God extirpated absolutely by force. Why? Because he found the Motherland and is quite happy about it." To satisfy his need of the absolute, Christianity offered splendid prospects and a high ideal, well worth the attention of all his energies.

Merejikovsky will say that the Western genius is in moderation and the Russian genius is in excess. Western people can stop in time; when they meet barriers, they go around them, or they return in their own footsteps. When Russians make a start, they never stop; they do not walk, they fly; they break all barriers, or break their own necks against them.

How can this passionate impulse, this latent energy, be reconciled with the passivity, indolence, sensibility, and sweetness that seem to be characteristic features of the Slavic soul?

It is because the Russian decides to act only when he sees the reason or the justification of his action; he has instinctive contempt for contingent and imperfect aims; he needs an unquestionable imperative, he seeks true values of life, and the ultimate meaning of things. The strength of Slavics, so writes Soloviev, is that we do not spend our energies in inferior spheres of activity. In a country of unlimited sky, open to every invader, crossed by all the migrations of history, man is conscious of his weakness, of the perishable nature of his work, and concentrates his affection on what cannot be taken away from him, his interior life, his spiritual liberty, the worship of his ancestors, feelings shared by the community, familial and national love, and at the last his faith. The more cruel his life, the greater will be his aloofness from the contingent, his trend to the transcendent, his desire to be united to God.

This aloofness does not mean at all, as explained by Berdiaev, that the Russian is less sinful than other people, but he is wicked in another way. It is by his sins that he will be attached to the things of this earth, and not by his virtues, or by his notion of truth and justice, or by his ideal of sanctity. In fact, Western man is fond of his social position, of his belongings, of his comfort in life, not by reason of his weaknesses and vices, but on account of his social virtues founded on and justified by religion. But the Russian is by no means seriously convinced of the sacredness of his property, or that the enjoyment of the pleasures of life is justified and in accordance with the leading of a perfect life.

The Russian is wholly conscious that the present world is not his permanent city; he fixes his gaze on the city of the future. In a sense, it is true to state that no other people in the world expects with such intensity the glorious final advent of Christ, the transfiguration of the world, and the final triumph of the good. A great Messianic expectation is concealed in Russian spiritual life, and this is why the Easter Festival Day is so particularly loved by the Russian people. For them it is not merely the commemoration of the resurrection of Christ, mystically relived; it is the expectation of the cosmic resurrection, the resurrection and glorification of the entire created world. The Russian believer is already turned toward the light spread by the one who will come to fulfill the promise of glorification and transfiguration and to establish the kingdom of God.

The fervent Russian worship of our Lady is also marked by this vision of the world. Old Russian iconography expressed in pictures the canticle to Mary, "Every creature rejoices in thee, full of grace." We see the Mother of God surrounded not only by angels and men, but also by the sun, the stars, plants, birds, and all creatures. The Blessed Virgin appears as a symbol of the true relation of each creature with the Creator. Better than any other word, the *Fiat* of the Virgin expresses absolute dependence on God, which is the true essence of man and all created beings; it indicates the availability of divinity and supernatural transfiguration. The assumption of the body of the Blessed Virgin is in some way a pledge of the liberation of the universe, already begun and being realized on this earth. While the atheists hope that this transfiguration will be effected solely by human and natural forces, which means that they expect it to come from the material forces that have produced man, the Blessed Virgin shows us by her *Fiat* the surest way toward transfiguration which comes from above, by virtue of the divine mercy.

If this transfiguration must be effected by a miracle rather than by the historical evolution of humanity, we can understand why the Russian people indulge in nihilistic opinions when they forget God. Not so much attached as the Western people to the values of civilization, they consider that everything is permitted if they do not have faith in God and in the immortality of the soul. The object of these desires will always be the same: salvation, liberation, new life. But as he does not notice any evolutionary means toward this new world, the Russian tries to discover a radical remedy, apart from anything temporal; he wants to conduct a cosmic revolution in order that a new life may start. Even in the Russian atheist, Christian motives can be found at the bottom of his being. During the past war, some young Russian volunteers took as a motto the following lines of a Russian writer: "The most precious thing for a man is life. It is only given to him once and he must live his life in such a way that at his death he may say: my whole life and strength have been devoted to the most wonderful thing in the world: the struggle for the liberation of humanity."

The idea of general salvation is intimately connected with the idea of the transfiguration of the world: if one man is to be saved, it is in common with all and not separately. Dostoevski will say that all are responsible for all. All souls are united, and no one goes to God without leading others on: "Save yourself, and thousands around you will be saved." This feature of spiritual collectivism, this aspiration to the general salvation of the people, of humanity, and of the whole world, is common to the Russian way of thinking, to believers or the incredulous, to the Slavish friends as well as to the promoters of the Russian revolution. Nadson writes: "As long as there will be tears in the world, as long as the darkness shall not be pierced, the concerns and dreams of personal happiness are infinitely shameful." But this characteristic feature of the Russian soul will be found above all in the Russian saints, where its true supernatural greatness will be reached. Even the most mystical of them will not disinterest themselves from the lot of their neighbor or of the world. Having reached far away from the world, in union with God, they will come back and bring mankind the message of salvation. The Russian mystic, although deep with great internal intensity, is at the same time very active and ready to fight evil wherever it may be.

The director of Alyosha Karamazof sends the monk out into the world and tells him: "Act, act! Love your fellow creatures in a practical way; all the glory and merit of man are to be found in the practice of charity. Today you act for the first time. Henceforth you will extend your field of action. Today you devote yourself to your brother; tomorrow devote yourself to your family, and after that to your Motherland, and then finally to humanity."

The phenomenon of latent forces ripening in solitude and ultimately intended to be devoted to the world, does not seem to be characteristic of only a few monks and saints, but of the whole Russian people. In the nineteenth century, many Russian thinkers had the intuition of a preparatory stage of apostolic enlightenment in Russia that, after a deep spiritual crisis, would affect the world. This is confirmed by writers who have a good knowledge of Russia. Wilbois writes, for instance: "It seems that Russia's solitude was of no other use to her than to develop qualities intended to shine later on. God has separated Russia from the world during ten centuries, with the purpose of handing her over to the world in the eleventh. Her fate is twofold. We are now at the point of returning from the retreat to the apostolate."

Especially during the past years signs of religious renewal have been evident. Cardinal Tisserant said: "Signs of religious disquietude are more frequently observed nowadays in Russia than before. Proof is in the fact that the newspaper of Komsomol complains fairly often that the members of Communist youth are not faithful to their rules; they go to church even though it is forbidden, and are married religiously in spite of their membership in the Party. A great religious flowering may be hoped for in the future of Russia."

No later than the April 20, 1958, *Pravda* complained that not only old and ignorant persons, but also engineers, geologists, and the like were attracted by the pilgrimage to Zagorsk with its miraculous relic of St. Sergius. Paradoxically, perhaps, the privation of God is an excellent preparation for appreciating the gift of Christian faith, as has often been testified. One who reads the Gospel for the first time after having reached the age of an adult, and after having anxiously considered all the problems of life, may admire the divine wisdom shining in these pages even more than a believer accustomed to the beauties of the Gospel. Boris Pasternak, author of the novel *Doctor Zhivago*, a best seller, declared formally: "I do not believe in the materialistic dialectic. I believe in God. Centuries are degrees for the steps of God." He writes in his novel, "To make history is to base one's self on profane works in order to resolve little by little the problem of death and to overreach it in the future. . . . To make discoveries of this kind, one needs spiritual tools, and in this sense all data are already contained in the Gospel. Here they are: First of all the love of neighbor. . . . Then the essential reasons for man today, without which he is unthinkable, i.e., the ideal of a free personality and of life conceived as a sacrifice. The Forefathers had no history in this sense. It is only since Christ that the centuries and generations have breathed freely."

Every day witnesses the increase in the number of those who discover again the way of faith, guided by the beauty of creation, or by the discovery of their soul. "By the star-spangled sky, and by my soul, Thou assertest that Thou exist," writes the poet Klenoski, and he proceeds, "as the child born blind who has never seen the visage of his mother, yet he remembers the sweet murmur, the song, the caress of an affectionate hand, the warmth and an endless tenderness; in the same way, without seeing Thee, I too know Thee, in spite of earthly reason; I perceive Thy breath, I hear Thy song, I understand Thy murmur, I feel the sweetness of Thy hand." He feels immediately the need of telling his discovery to all those who are waiting: "Everyone must share the knowledge acquired, and it is now our turn to give others the promise of the coming joy."

It would, therefore, be false to believe that, with Russians, detachment from the things of this world relates to indifference for humanity, as a result of a disincarnated charity. "To be a Russian," so writes Dostoevski, "only means to be the brother of all men." Wilbois says the same: "If charity is the fundamental law of Christianity, Russian blood is Christian."

Numerous and recent testimonies to this effect may be found, without referring to the evidence given by several prisoners and foreigners who have come back from Russia.

Still, the affective intensity of the Russian soul can be badly orientated, even if it cannot be taken away without being destroyed. By reason of his impulsive and less rational temperament, the Russian becomes violent more easily than another. We know of sufficiently numerous unfortunate instances of this. But the Christian message is powerful enough to transform a violent and even criminal soul: Alyosha Kamarazof does not escape the hereditary violence, but "this force is completely orientated in him toward the good; in this force exists a Faith which moves mountains" (Dostoevski). Thus, the paradox of charity with violence is reconciled the same as that of dynamism with passivity referred to above.

The influence of Christianity was deeply felt in the creativity effected in all branches of culture. The Russian people are essentially artistic, and music, poetry, literature, iconography, and choreography have always played a great part in Russian life. In the nineteenth century, the growing young Russian culture asserted itself as a religious culture; only by its religious motives was it national. One finds in it an ascetic tendency that is never fascinated by the worship of pleasure. The interest manifested today in Russia in the literature of the nineteenth century is strong evidence for this point of view.

The Christian vision of the world cannot be separated from the worship of ethical beauty which appears like a lively and not an abstract truth. We find here again the Greek concept *kalokagathos* and the concept of ethical beauty as a motive of action. Rosanov writes, for instance: "Great beauty makes us indifferent to anything ordinary and everything is ordinary when compared to Jesus Christ."

This was a peculiarity of Eastern Christianity that inspired the Russian people, and it was based on the idea that liturgical and iconographical beauty is intended to be a kind of revelation of the beauty of God that a Christian must find reproduced again in creatures. To a loving eye, spiritually transfigured, the world also appears transfigured, and the beauty of God is seen in creatures. Everything is transformed in the splendor of the Incarnation and Redemption of Christ. Such is the basic idea of the Orthodox Church, writes Arseniev, when he explains the sympathy of the Russian for St. Francis of Assisi, who embodies exactly this essential aspect of Eastern Christianity.

This taste for the beautiful, intrinsic to the Russian soul, incurs a real danger, however; that of being fascinated by the appearance of beauty, by a false mystique. The Russian easily believes what suits him, what seems to correspond to his intimate longings. He is not skeptical by nature. "Anything considered as hypothetical in the Westerner, becomes an axiom for us," said Dostoevski. The lack of a critical spirit may translate itself into a lack of discernment, and bring the Russian to adopt errors with great fervor.

Everything said so far will help us to understand another contradiction of the Russian soul: its exuberant joy and the melancholy of its songs. There is this longing for the plenitude of life. To live fully you must rejoice in your existence. The Russian soul longs for a religion that brings it joy. The central event of Christianity is the good news of the coming of the Son of God into this world. If, since the Old Testament, the whole earth is called to rejoice, what ought we to say of the redeemed Christians, those who were sanctified by the passion and resurrection of Christ who promised to remain with them until the end of time? "Yes, God is with us," writes Soloviev. "He is here present among the vain tumults, in the troubled brook of human anxiety, and you carry in yourself the joyous mystery; the evil is powerless, we are eternal, God is with us."

But what will be the fate of this joy when it faces the unavoidable trials of life? To simply state them is not a complete answer, because the Eastern heathens also easily accepted the pains they attributed to the malicious interference of a god or fate. The love of pain is the Christian answer to God. Life is too wonderful, even at its most painful hours, to be simply accepted: one cannot resign oneself before a masterpiece. "The Russian people belong to the small number of those that love the essence of Christianity, namely the Cross" (Leroy-Beaulieu). "Everything is atoned for by suffering," says Dostoevski. "It is a good thing." A poet puts it in these words: "The darker the night, the brighter are the stars; the deeper the pain, the nearer to God."

The story of the Russian people is a story of pain and crucifixion. The Russian is naturally accustomed to suffering. Christianity will only sublimate this habit, by showing him in future happiness the marvelous transfiguration of his suffering: "All tears will shine like diamonds on the mantle of the Mother of God . . . and the one who follows the Lord on the way he passed himself, understands the greatness of the kingdom of Heaven," said Empress Alexandria. Suffering is also caused by personal sins: the Russian is aware that he is a sinner; he judges himself severely and willingly does penance. Throughout his story, he is never satisfied with himself. The best critical comments were formulated by the Russians themselves, and if the word "auto-critic" is a recent one, the process is old.

In a nutshell it may be said that Christianity had a brightening influence on the Russian soul, which appears at its best in the Russian saints; they are better balanced, more joyful, and more charitable for it all.

It is a pleasure to be able to associate myself, in the name of the Christians of Russia, with this tribute paid by all continents, and to express my best wishes for a new Pentecost that shall bring all the separated brethren into the unity of the Church. It would be a splendid achievement requiring the co-operation of all because, as it was stated by Soloviev, big things cannot be effected by small means. A climate of understanding, an intellectual and moral link must be found between the religious conscience of the Eastern Christians and the universal truth of the Catholic Church. The true beauty of Western Christianity must be revealed to them. Why must all valuable works be translated in the Russian language by earnest atheists, while Catholic thought is almost completely ignored?

Why must refugees from the East complain that they live for years in Catholic surroundings without being initiated to common religious problems? If the message of Fatima gave birth to a hope in our hearts, is it not that we may become free co-operators with God in the fulfillment of His merciful designs? Soloviev terminates the prologue of his work, *Russia and the Universal Church,* with these words, which will also terminate my address: "A race full of strength and desires but without clear consciousness of its destiny knocks on the door of universal history. Let them come in, key bearer of Christ, that the door of history might be for them and for the world the door to the Kingdom of God."

CHINA

BY DR. JOHN CHING-HSIUNG WU (PREFERABLY JOHN C. H. WU) . . . *Born, March 28, 1899, in Ningpo-China.* POLITICAL CAREER: *judge and chief justice of Provisional Court of Shanghai, International Settlement (1927–1929); member of National Legislature of China (1933–1946); adviser to Chinese delegation to United Nations Conference, San Francisco, 1945; minister plenipotentiary of China to Holy See (1947–1949); nominated by Chinese Nationalist Government and designated by United Nations as member of UN panel for inquiry and conciliation of international controversies (1950—); member of Permanent Court of Arbitration at the Hague (1957—).* ACADEMIC CAREER: *LL.B., Comparative Law School of China, 1920; J.D., University of Michigan Law School, 1921; Research Fellow, University of Paris (1921–1922); Research Fellow, University of Berlin (1922–1923); Research Scholar, Harvard University Law School (1923–1924); professor of Law, Comparative School of China (1924–1939); principal of same (1927–1939); Rosenthal lecturer, Northwestern University Law School (winter, 1929); Research Fellow (as faculty member), Harvard University Law School (spring, 1930); honorary member, American Academy of Sciences and Art (1939—); visiting senior professor of Chinese Philosophy, University of Hawaii (1949–1951); honorary life member, New York Guild of Catholic Lawyers (1951); professor of Law, Seton Hall University, New Jersey (1951—); LL.D., Boston College, 1953; LL.D., University of Portland.* PUBLICATIONS: Juridical Essays and Studies *(Shanghai, 1928);* The Art of Law *(Shanghai, 1936);* Beyond East and West *(New York, 1951);* The Interior Carmel *(New York, 1953);* Fountain of Justice *(1955)*

A beautiful affair was the wedding feast in Cana. Our Lady was there, and so were Jesus and His disciples. A festive mood was in the air, and who can blame the guests if they drank more than usual? Perhaps they should have remembered that the newly wedded were of moderate means. But to remain temperate on such a happy occasion would be an instance of immoderate moderation. The Oriental temper would not have allowed it. The fact remains that the supply of wine failed when the spirits of the guests were running high. You can hardly imagine what a terrible embarrassment it was for the bridegroom and bride. Our Lady, herself an Oriental, knew what a serious "loss of face" such an untoward event would mean for a new couple. It would remain on their memory like an unsightly scar, thus marring their marital happiness.

Impelled by her unbounded human sympathy, our Lady rose to the occasion. Knowing that only her Son could save the situation, she approached Him in the ladylike manner so characteristic of her, not by making a direct request, but by passing on to Him information pregnant with suggestion: "They have no wine." Our Lord gave her a gentle rebuff. "What wouldst thou have me do? My hour has not yet come," He said. This was the fore-echo, as it were, of that heart-rending prayer He was to utter three years later in the garden of Gethsemani: "Father, if it is possible, let this cup pass away from me" (Mt. 26:39). *True Man* as He is, how could He help feeling afflicted even at the start of a journey that was to lead to Calvary? Did His Mother realize this as clearly as He did? I wonder. But being *true God*, could He help being divinely pleased by His Mother's marvelous spirit of charity, which, unimpeded by the barriers of sin, flowed out spontaneously from her Immaculate Heart toward all children of man, especially the poor and needy? Nor was she discouraged by His rebuff; she went ahead to tell the waiters, "Whatever he shall say to you, do ye."

Now it happened that there were six stone waterpots standing there, as the Jewish custom of ceremonial washing demanded. Jesus, accommodating Himself to what was already there, said to the waiters, "Fill the jars with water." After they had filled each of them up to the brim, Jesus said to them, "Draw out now, and take to the chief steward," which they did accordingly.

In the meantime, the water had been transformed into wine, and when the chief steward tasted it, not knowing whence it had come, he called the bridegroom and said to him, "Every man at first sets forth the good wine, and when they have drunk freely, then that which is poorer. But thou hast kept the good wine until now" (Jn. 2:10).

For the purposes of my present discourse, the six waterpots stand for the six cardinal relations of men, as the Chinese ethical tradition has presented them. Confucius and other sages of old China have filled them almost to the brim with the water of natural wisdom, waiting only for us to do the rest and for Christ to turn it into wine.

Now, what are the six cardinal relations of men according to the natural philosophy of the Chinese sages? Ordinarily, only five relations are mentioned explicitly, namely, father and son, elder brother and younger brother, husband and wife, friend and friend, prince and minister. But in reality there is a sixth, which is implicitly assumed when the Chinese scholars speak of human relations; and that is the relation between the teacher and the pupil. In fact, this last relation was regarded as of transcending importance. To quote from a Confucian classic, "The drum has no special relation to any of the five musical notes; but without it they cannot be harmonized. Water has no special relation to any of the five colors; but without it they cannot be displayed. Learning is not specially related to any of the five senses but without it they cannot be regulated. The teacher lies outside of the five degrees of mourning; but without his guidance human relations would be devoid of the appropriate affection." The teacher, therefore, may be compared to the conductor of the whole symphony of human relations. But it would take too long to enlarge upon the functions of the teacher, so I shall confine myself to the other relations.

1. Father and Son. In the Chinese classics very little can be found on the duties of parents toward their children, the emphasis being on the duties of children toward their parents. In no other culture to my knowledge has the philosophy of filial piety been so well developed as in China. Herein lies both the strength and weakness of Chinese culture.

Confucius himself had a rather balanced conception of filial piety. On one occasion he is reported to have said to a ruler, "A man of true humanity serves his parents as Heaven, and serves Heaven as his parents" (*Li Chi*, Ai Kung Wen). But later Confucianists, beginning already with his disciple Tseng Sheng, developed the first part of this remarkable statement to the point of hypertrophy, leaving the second part to atrophy almost completely. In the system of Confucius, filial piety was the starting point of all virtues, with humanity (*jen*) as the ultimate virtue embracing all the others. He himself was a filial child of Heaven, to whose will he became more and more docile as he grew in years. That is why he said that at fifty he had begun to know the will of Heaven, and at sixty his ears had become attuned to the biddings of Heaven.

When we come to the teachings of his disciple Tseng Sheng, we find an altogether different atmosphere. Tseng Sheng was a good man with a narrow mental outlook. His outstanding virtue was that of filial piety toward his parents. But his ethical philosophy lacks the catholicity and balance and palpitating richness which we find in that of Confucius. He makes filial piety not only the starting point, but also the sum total of all virtues. Thus, in his system, filial piety takes the place occupied by humanity in the system of his master.

Tseng Sheng's philosophy of life, like his character, has the charm of a rugged simplicity. He derived all virtues from filial piety. The underlying reason of our duty of filial love and gratitude toward our parents is that we owe our very body to our parents, and therefore we must hold the body as a sacred trust from them. In Tseng Sheng's own words, "The body itself being something transmitted to us from our parents, how dare we be careless in the employment of our legacy?" (*Li Chi*, Chi Yi.) From this fundamental intuition follow all our other duties, such as self-respect, loyalty to the ruler, faithfulness to our friends, conscientiousness in discharging our public functions, in one word, assiduous self-cultivation in all things; for all our attainments and achievements will redound to the glory of our parents, as surely as our failing and lack of character will cast discredit on them.

As you can easily imagine, this was a very practical and down-to-earth philosophy of life, which anyone with average intelligence and strength of character could grasp and make his own. It is little wonder that throughout the later generations up to the beginning of this century this philosophy should have been the dominating feature of the mental landscape of Chinese scholars in general. It furnished the main motive to all their actions. It instilled a meaning to their existence and made life worth living for them.

But this family-centered philosophy of life has its serious drawbacks, if it is not balanced by the idea of brotherhood of men under the Fatherhood of God. Catholicism preserves the sound kernel of the idea of family solidarity, but at the same time it does not make a god of the family head, as Confucianism has tended to do. In other words, Christianity, while emphasizing the duty of filial piety, does not allow it to degenerate into clanishness. The teachings of Christ and St. Paul subordinate filial piety on the natural plane under that higher filial piety which we owe to the Father of all. Christ's filial love for His Mother lasted up to the very end of His life on earth. I need only remind you of His words spoken from the Cross to St. John: "Behold thy mother," and to His Mother: "Woman, behold thy son." How tenderly He loved His Mother! But this did not prevent Him from attending to His "Father's business" and fulfilling His supreme mission of redemption of mankind. Nor did Mary's motherly love prevent her from being the co-redemptrix.

I do not wish to be understood as maintaining that the Chinese cultivation of filial piety has nothing to contribute to the lives of many Christians. It does not add anything new to Christianity, but to modern Christians it should serve as a reminder of the fourth Commandment, which, as St. Paul pointed out in special emphasis, "is the first commandment with a promise: That it may be well with thee, and thou mayest be longlived upon the earth" (Eph. 6:1–3). One wonders if the individualistic philosophy of the past few centuries in the West has not eclipsed this important Commandment in the lives of Christians.

In their practice of filial piety the ancient Chinese went to heroic lengths. They may have gone a little too far. But some of the moral intuitions uttered by Confucius in this regard belong to the perennial philosophy of mankind. Let us be contented with a couple of instances. When a disciple asked Confucius how to serve one's parents, the master answered, "According to the modern ideas, filial piety consists in providing the parents with enough to eat. But even dogs and horses are cared for to that extent. If there is no feeling of respect, where is the distinction between the two?" Another disciple asked the same question and Confucius said, "The difficulty is with the countenance. Merely to toil and labor for the old folks and to furnish them with wine and food is not the sum total of filial piety. Is it?" (*Lun Yu*, 2:7 and 8.) But why did he lay such stress on the "countenance"? Because the countenance is the index to the interior feeling. The interior feeling is the kernel, but the kernel that must grow into a complete fruit. In another classic, we find an elucidation of this point. "When the love of a filial son goes really deep, he will naturally possess a spirit of harmony; when he has the spirit of harmony, he will naturally radiate an atmosphere of gladness; when he has the atmosphere of gladness, his countenance and manners will have a spontaneous charm and grace about them" (*Li Chi*, Chi I). The moral system of Confucius is as practical and matter-of-fact as the Rule of St. Benedict.

Sometimes I think that if only we Christians could serve God with as much sincerity and preparation, as much love and reverence, as many of the Confucian scholars have served their parents, we should really be saints. The greatness of Dom Celestine Lou lay precisely in this, that he had absorbed the whole spirit of filial piety as taught by Confucius and applied it, with the help of the grace and example of Christ, to the serving and loving of our Heavenly Father. In the meantime, he continued to love his country and his parents, not in place of God, but in Him and through Him. Whenever I think of Dom Lou, I remember something that St. Therese said: "A heart given to God loses nothing of its natural affection;

on the contrary, that affection grows stronger by becoming purer and more spiritual" (*The Story of a Soul*, Chap. 9).

By "father and son," the Chinese really meant "parent and child," thus including the mother and the daughter. In the history of China I do not know how many great men owed their upbringing to their mothers. The mother of Mencius, for instance, believed that the education of a child should begin in the womb, and she acted upon her belief. She was the Chinese counterpart of St. Monica, who wept for the sins of her son more bitterly than other mothers weep for the bodily deaths of their children (cf. *St. Augustine's Confessions*, a new translation by Sheed, p. 42). In the end he became doubly her child, the child of her blood and of her tears.

2. Brothers. From the relation of parent and child, we pass on to that of brothers. A Chinese regards his brothers as members of his own body. The elder brother normally exercises a protective love over the younger, and the latter looks to the former with a kind of deferential affection. Of course, even in ancient China there were quarrels between brothers. But on the whole I believe that there was a greater sense of solidarity between brothers in China than in any other country. Let me quote a realistic stanza from an ancient song:

Within the walls brothers may fight,
But insults from without
Will their forces and hearts unite
The common foe to rout.

Even after brothers had married and established families of their own, they usually made visits to each other. The commonest feeling has been expressed by a well-known couplet:

Every time we see each other we have grown older.
How many more years can we remain brothers?

The idea is that one lifetime is hardly enough in which to enjoy being brothers. A most famous pair of brothers were Su Tung-po and Su Tse-yu. Both of them were consummate writers, whose essays are still found in contemporary anthologies. They uttered together a joint wish: "May we remain brothers throughout all the future transmigrations of our souls!" This is indeed a beautiful wish based upon the Buddhist faith. The faith may be illusory, as I believe it is, but who will gainsay the intensity of affection as expressed by the tremendous wish?

All this is very beautiful, but I have come to know some pairs of Christian brothers whose story is even more beautiful. A few years ago I was thrilled in receiving a letter from a seminarian in Loyola Villa in Wisconsin. I take the liberty of quoting a few lines from it: "I am a Jesuit of some four years now. My vocation came after I had completed my college and had already embarked on my chosen calling, the Law. I accredit this *volte-face* (not really that the vocations are incompatible, but rather the one incorporates the other) to the prayers of my twin brother who entered the year previous." I usually do not quote from private letters, but this event is too joyful to be kept to myself. How deeply these brothers must love each other!

But not all brothers need to be twins or priests in order to feel the redoubling of their affection. When our Lord used me as an instrument for the conversion of my elder brother and my elder sister, I felt, in addition to the natural fraternal affection, a kind of maternal tenderness for them. I told our Lord, "Now I have borne you some big children, haven't I?" When I converted some of my elder children, I felt that now I was not only their father but also their mother. Sometimes I feel like a younger brother of my children when my faults are discovered by them.

3. Husband and Wife. From brothers let us pass on to an even more interesting relation, husband and wife. The marriage ceremony of old China was perhaps the most solemn outside of the Catholic Church. But I remember what an old Confucian scholar said to me after attending my eldest son's nuptial Mass in Shanghai. Archbishop Paul Yupin was the celebrant, and the late Father Beda Chang gave a sermon. And the old Confucian scholar was so deeply impressed by the solemnities that he remarked, "This is exactly what our old marital rites foreshadowed!" In other words, the seeds that Confucianism had sown came into flowering in the Sacrament of Marriage.

In China the good wishes of our friends at our marriage were expressed in some such phrases as: "Wish you two grow old together and live to see gray hairs on each other's head!" "Wish you two to see your children and grandchildren fill your hall!" "This union is made by Heaven!" "May you always love each other like a pair of mandarin ducks!"

All these sentiments and ideals are embodied in the Catholic *marriage service*, in the *blessing*, and in the *nuptial Mass*.

And from this we may perceive that all that man by nature could legitimately wish and desire has a place in the liturgy of the Church. One thing noteworthy is that the Church liturgy seems to be more matter-of-fact than the Chinese counterparts. For the Chinese did not like to mention such things as "death," "sickness," or even "poverty" at such an auspicious occasion as marriage. In fact, "grow old together" was the limit of proprieties, for it was a euphemism of death. The Church could afford to call a spade a spade, because of the assurance of a higher hope.

Two things are missing in the Chinese ceremony. One is "What therefore God hath joined together, let no man put asunder." As you know, in certain cases, the old Chinese law permitted a husband to put away his wife, although this privilege was but rarely exercised. The other element which is missing in the Chinese ceremony is the most significant factor of a Christian marriage; it is bodied forth in this expression: "O God, who hast hallowed wedlock by a mystery so excellent that in the marriage bond Thou didst foreshadow the union of Christ with the Church." This is the keynote that makes the Christian marriage a Sacrament. The Catholic couple are not only one flesh but one spirit. They are two hands folded together in eternal adoration.

In the normal marital life in old China, the man and wife did not know each other, at least not intimately, before their wedding; but gradually as they had children their hearts were more and more united by a common love; and finally they became lovers as their friendship grew. This is the direct opposite of modern romantic love. Today, when two young persons meet and court each other, their love immediately reaches the boiling point. The boy looks like an archangel, and the girl looks like a goddess. Then they marry and discover each other to be only human beings full of frailties and perhaps selfishness. When an illusion is shattered, there comes disenchantment. From disenchantment comes resentment. In such a state, one is most vulnerable to new illusions, whose false splendors make the realities appear even more miserable. To the romantics, marriage is, in theory and in practice, the "grave of love." Many nominal Christians are romantics in actual practice if not in theory. But the true Catholic philosophy of love is similar to the Chinese philosophy, in that it considers the wedding as the starting point of love and marital life as a school of love. Only it is far superior to the latter because the common love in a Catholic family is not only the children but God. Furthermore, while good Catholics would consult their parents on the choice of their spouses, the final decision rests with them, and not with parents, who only do the counseling.

But even outside of the Church, marital love is meant to be a lifelong romance, when things go in the normal way. I have seen a number of old couples in China living happily like pairs of nuthatches sticking together until the end.

4. The Relationship of Friendship. So far we have been dealing with family relations, strictly so called. But all human relations aspire to friendship just as all arts aspire to music.

In the history of China there have been innumerable instances of exemplary friendship between man and man. But not the least beautiful is the friendship between Po Ya, the most famous lute player of ancient China, and his great *connoisseur*, Chung Tse Ch'i. Although Po Ya was admired by the whole world, yet no one else knew the inward vision that inspired his art. On one happy occasion, Chung Tse Ch'i was among his listeners. As he played on the lute, his mind roamed to the high mountains. At the end of the performance, Chung Tse Ch'i exclaimed, "O how sublime! The music soared to the sky like the mountain ridges!" When Po Ya played the next piece, his thoughts were wafted to the flowing streams. Chung Tse Ch'i again exclaimed, "O how beautiful! The sound has ended, but the music goes on like an ever flowing river!"

Other people appreciated the sound of the music; Chung Tse Ch'i alone saw the inner landscape of the musician. They became bosom friends. But, unfortunately, Chung Tse Ch'i died shortly afterward. Po Ya felt the bereavement so keenly that he cut off the strings and broke the lute. He never played again for the rest of his life.

This touching story portrays the Chinese idea of friendship. In fact, up to now, we speak of a friend as *chi yin*, which means "the *connoisseur* of our music." It is to our friends that we pour out our hearts in full strains. For, as Christ Himself has told us, it would be foolish to "cast your pearls before swine, lest perhaps they trample them under their feet, and turning upon you they tear you" (Mt. 7:6).

The minimum condition of friendship is that two hearts must meet somewhere. If your heart is set on heavenly things and mine on the things of the world, then we keep our treasures in different places, and there can be no meeting of minds between us. There is a hierarchy of friendships. The lowest order is one which is based upon a common material interest. Much higher is one based upon common moral principles. Still higher is the sharing together of a noble vision.

Of all his students, Confucius had a very special friendship for Yen Hui, because their hearts were perfectly united in a common philosophy of values, and their minds in a common vision. First of all they shared in a sincere love of wisdom. Confucius spoke of himself that "in a hamlet of ten houses, there must be some who are just as loyal and faithful as myself, but there is none who loves learning and wisdom as I do." He once told a friend that among his students there was only one true lover of learning and wisdom, Yen Hui, but that unfortunately he was dead. Because they loved wisdom for its own sake, and not as a means to worldly riches or position, they did not mind being poor. Confucius was deeply impressed by Yen Hui's detachment from such things. He once exclaimed, "What a virtuous man is Hui! A single bowl of millet, a single ladle of soup, living in a mean alley! Others felt sorry for him, but Hui himself remained as cheerful as ever! What a remarkable man!" (*The Analects*, 6:11.) Speaking of himself, Confucius said, "With coarse food to eat, water for drink, and a bent arm for a pillow, I could find happiness even in such a state. As for wealth and honor improperly obtained, they are to me like a fleeting cloud" (7:15).

But most important of all, they had in common a childlike confidence in Providence. Once as Confucius was traveling with a group of his students in a foreign state, they were surrounded by threatening forces sent by the ruler on account of some misunderstanding. Confucius continued to play his lute and sing as if nothing were happening. Everybody was scandalized by his spirit of *insouciance*, but not Yen Hui. Confucius called them one by one and put to each of them the same question, as a test: "An old ode has it: 'We are not rhinoceroses, we are not tigers. How is it that we find ourselves roaming the wilds?' Now, tell me, is it because our Way is wrong? Why has it brought us to this pass?" After receiving a few answers, which showed how little the pupils saw eye to eye with him, he called in Yen Hui, and put to him the same question. Yen Hui said, "Your Way is extremely great. That is why the world cannot contain it, but this is no cause for worry. Precisely because the world cannot contain and tolerate our Way, we are assured that it is a noble Way. The trouble is with the world, not with the Way." Confucius smiled affably and said, "Son of Yen family! I wish you were a wealthy man. In that case, I would like to be your steward." Yen Hui was to Confucius what Chung Tse Ch'i was to Po Ya.

One of the qualities of friendship on which the Chinese sages have laid the greatest emphasis is that of constancy and permanence in the face of the vicissitudes of life. Here again we find the fulfillment in Christ, who, having loved His own during His life on earth, "loved them unto the end." What is more, the end is only a beginning.

It is important to point out that there is nothing static or exclusive about friendship. No, it is dynamic and expansive. In the end, friendship merges into the Confucian virtue of humanity, which is the natural counterpart of Christian charity. Confucius described the virtue of humanity in these terms: "Being established yourself in the way of truth, you wish to help others to be likewise established.

Having thoroughly understood the way of truth, you wish to help others to attain the same understanding. To be able from one's own self to draw a parallel for the treatment of others may be called the art of humanity" (*The Analects*, 6).

Now, this comes pretty close to the Christian initiative in the making of friends. It has been said that the only way to make a friend is to be one. A true apostle, whether priestly or lay, offers his friendship to every man. He is everybody's friend without becoming "nobody's friend." The secret is that having the friendship of our Lord, he loves all men as He does, but does not rest his happiness upon being understood and loved by them.

This is the summit of the Christian ideal of life. But before we reach the summit, there is a great need of friends who can help each other in the climb. There is a touching scene between two disciples of Confucius, which may edify us. Tse Hsia lost his son and was so overwhelmed by grief he lost his eyesight. Tseng Sheng came to console him, saying, "As I have heard, when a friend loses his eyesight, we should lament for him." As Tseng Sheng started wailing, Tse Hsia also wailed and in a moment of anguish he said, "O Heaven, wherein have I offended?" Upon hearing this complaint, Tseng Sheng was moved to anger, and said to him, "How can you say that you have not offended. You and I served the Master between the two streams, Chu and Hsi, but after his death you retired and grew old in the neighborhood of the Western River, where you made the people compare you with the Master. This was one offense. When you lost your parents, people heard nothing about it. This was your second offense. When you lost your son, you mourned so much that you lost your eyesight. This is your third offense. And yet you say, 'Wherein have I offended?'" Tse Hsia threw down his staff and bowed, saying, "I was wrong, I was wrong. It is a long time since I isolated myself from the community of my friends and lived all alone here."

5. Prince and Minister. On this relationship hangs a whole system of political philosophy. I can only touch upon one of its problems here, namely, the foundation of political authority. With all his respect for authority, Confucius was no positivist or absolutist.

To him, political authority is not based upon force, but upon virtue. Theoretically, he justified this doctrine by the logic of names or concepts. But in reality his logic is saturated with ethical connotations. For example, he declared that the prince, to be worthy of the name, should behave like a true prince, and the minister, to be worthy of the name, should behave like a true minister. He held that the root of all evils in his time was that the prince is not like a prince, the minister not like a minister, the father not like a father, the son not like a son. This way of employing names or concepts as rule and measure of realities is akin to St. Paul's way when he wrote to Timothy to "honor widows who are truly widowed." For "she who gives herself up to pleasures is dead while she is still alive" (1 Tim. 5:3 and 6).

In other words, the mere physical fact that a person held the position of a prince is not enough to make him a prince in the proper sense of the term. A prince, properly so called, must possess princely virtue. Confucius was emphatic on this point. To be a ruler, one must be straight within oneself. A ruler who is not straight is a contradiction in terms. Confucius could be very brusque in his dealings with political superiors. Once a powerful officer, who was noted for corruption, came to consult Confucius as to how to cope with the rising tide of robberies and thefts. The answer of Confucius was: "If you yourself, sir, were not greedy, the people would not steal even for a reward."

Throughout the ages, the Confucian scholars have seldom failed to maintain their moral dignity vis-à-vis the sovereign and other political superiors. They were guided by the principles of justice and rectitude, sanctioned by their age-long tradition. They believed in the existence of an immutable moral law ordained by Heaven and therefore superior to the will of the king. For them, kingship and public offices were instituted for the well-being of the people, not for oppressing them. Once a king asked Mencius whether it was true that certain ancient kings were banished and overthrown by their ministers or subjects. Mencius answered, "So it is in the histories." "May, then, a subject put his sovereign to death?" asked the king. Mencius' reply was: "He who outrages humanity is called a robber;

and he who outrages justice is called a ruffian. The robber and ruffian we call a mere fellow. I have only heard of executing a mere fellow for his monstrous crimes, but I have not heard of murdering a monarch, in these instances" (*Works of Mencius*, Chin Hsin, 2). To him, "The noblest element in a country is the people; next in order come the Protecting Spirits of the land and grain; the lightest in the scale of importance is the ruler" (*ibid.*).

The Confucian scholars were respectful toward their sovereigns, but when moral issues were involved, they would sooner sacrifice their heads than compromise their principles. There have been a goodly number of martyrs of principle throughout the history of China. Let one instance suffice. In 1402, a famous Confucian scholar, Fang Hsiao-ju, was executed for refusing to draft rescripts for a usurping emperor. "You can kill me, but you cannot make me draft the rescripts." He threw the brush on the ground.

The philosophic faith which furnished the moral backbone to the Confucianists is presented in a nutshell in the words of Lu Ku'en (1538–1618): "There are only two things supreme in the world: One is Reason, the other Authority. Of the two, Reason is the more supreme. When one gives voice to Reason in the Imperial Court, even the Emperor cannot suppress it by his authority. And even when Reason is temporarily suppressed, it will always triumph in the end and will prevail in the world throughout the ages" (*Groaning Words*, Bk. 1, sec. 4).

We find the same philosophy, the same faith, and the same Spirit working in the modern martyrs in Asia as well as Europe. Let one instance suffice. Father John Tung, in opposing the Communist compaign to isolate the Catholics in China from the Mystical Body of Christ, declared, in a public speech, among other things, "I am today required to attack the representative of the Holy Father. Tomorrow I shall perhaps be forced to attack the representative of Jesus Christ, the Holy Father. The following day why should I not then be constrained to attack God Himself?" He further said, "If I live by deceit and fear death, I become a completely untrustworthy man, of use to no one. . . . I am a Catholic and desire to love both my country and my religion. I do not wish discord between the two, but if the government cannot work harmoniously with religion, persecution will follow and many victims will be demanded from among Catholics. In such an event it is better that I die right now."

Father Tung, like St. Thomas More, was the country's good citizen, but the Kingdom of God's first.

But there is a passage in Father Tung's speech which is peculiarly Chinese in flavor. "Gentlemen," he said, "I have but one soul, which I cannot share with you, but I have a body which may be divided. So it seems to me the best thing for me to do is to offer my soul in its entirety to God and His Holy Church, and my body to the country. If she should desire it, I will not refuse it to her. Good materialists, who deny the existence of the soul, cannot but be satisfied with the sacrifice of my body." The spirit is the spirit of a Christian martyr; the mode is the mode of a Chinese scholar. With Father John Tung, the waterpot has been filled to the brim, and Christ has turned it into wine. There is a prophetic note in Father Tung's speech, where he declared: "A Christian who is capable of denying his God, will be only too ready to betray his Church and his country. The Communists have a saying: 'For one man who falls ten thousand will rise.' And could a Catholic forget that the blood of martyrs is the seed of Christians?"

During the past fifteen years, I don't know how many holy priests and good Christians have been martyred by the red-handed butchers in my country and elsewhere, and how many are still waiting for their turn in jail. Truly this is the worst persecution that our much persecuted Church has ever suffered. But just as the persecution has been terrible so the harvest will be terrific. Of the conversion of my country there is absolutely no doubt in my mind. The important thing is for us survivors to live in the spirit of the martyrs, and to put every ounce of their energy into the great mission of spreading the reign of Christ in the hearts of all men.

Even before the Incarnation of His Son, God had created human nature and ennobled it by endowing it with the natural moral law appropriate to it. It is to the discovery and elaboration of this natural moral law that the Chinese philosophers have dedicated all their attention and energies. Their findings have not been entirely free from errors and exaggerations, but their efforts have not been vain. If the Greeks excelled in speculative philosophy, and the Romans excelled in jurisprudence, the Chinese have developed an ethical philosophy which is second to none outside of the Revealed Religion.

A. N. Whitehead, in his *Science and the Modern World,* has traced the marvelous development of modern scientific civilization to its origins in medieval Scholasticism. According to him, the habit of definite exact thought which made the scientific movement possible "was implanted in the European mind by the long dominance of scholastic logic and scholastic divinity." Speaking of Chinese civilization, Whitehead, while pointing out the lack of the above-mentioned tone and habit of thought as the principal cause of the meagerness of its scientific achievements, has nevertheless expressed a high appreciation of its other aspects. "For example," he wrote, "the more we know of Chinese art, Chinese literature, and the Chinese philosophy of life, the more we admire the heights to which that civilization attained. For thousands of years, there have been in China acute and learned men patiently devoting their lives to study. Having regard to the span of time, and to the population concerned, China forms the largest volume of civilization which the world has seen" (p. 6).

Time has come for Christian scholars to explore systematically the rich mine of natural wisdom of life in the cultures of China and other countries in the Orient, in order to "baptize" them as our medieval predecessors did with the Greek and Roman cultures. As Bishop Fulton Sheen has so well said, "The distance from nature to grace, from sin to salvation, from doubt to Faith, is the same for a Western soul as for the Eastern soul, for only Christ's grace can bridge the distance. From this point of view, Confucius can be just as good a starting point for the discovery of Our Divine Lord as Aristotle. It is conceivable that he may even be better, at least to the extent that his ethics is more personal, more intimate and existential. It would be a great mistake for our Western world to feel that the East must study Aristotle, before it can come to the Faith" (Introduction to Wu's *From Confucianism to Catholi-*

cism, p. 4). To this I wish only to add one more word. Although grace cannot dispense with nature, nature can fulfill its destiny only by receiving the blessings of grace and the leaven of the Spirit. Without the supernatural uplift, any natural system of ethics, however high it may be, tends inevitably to degenerate and to decay and die. As the chief steward of the feast so candidly put it, ordinarily people serve the better wine first and when the guests have well drunk they begin to serve the worse kind. Partly because of this inherent tendency of all things human, and partly because of our contact with the secularized part of the West, Chinese ethics has been rapidly decaying for more than a century. In the sage words of Celso Cardinal Costantini, we can only "conserve and deepen the ancient national Chinese culture by giving it the rejuvenation of Christianity." In so doing we are at the same time helping Christianity to fulfill its historical mission in the whole world.

INDIA

BY REV. FR. JEROME D'SOUZA, S.J. . . . *Born, 1897, at Moolky in South India; educated in St. Aloysius College, Mangalore, and at the Presidency College, Madras; lecturer at St. Joseph's College (1920); joined the Society of Jesus (1921); lived in many houses of the Society in France and Belgium; traveled extensively; professor, St. Joseph College, Trichinopoly (1933); principal and rector of the same; transferred to Loyola College, Madras (1942); appointed member of Indian delegation to United Nations General Assembly (1949); visiting professor of Fordham University; India's delegate to U.N.E.S.C.O. General Conference at New Delhi (1956); elected member of High Counsel of Society of Jesus (1957); broadcast frequently in India, France, Belgium, U.S.A., and Canada*

India is an entity, insofar as it is a single entity, of the utmost complexity. It presents such diversity of races, languages, and religions that it is reasonable to ask if there is a single Indian people of whose soul it is permissible to generalize. Writers speak of India not as one country but as a subcontinent. The political adversaries of India in former days, and those who are not sympathetic to her now, deny that there is an Indian nation at all. At best, they say, there is an agglomeration of nations differing among themselves more than the nations of Europe differ among themselves, bound together by a strong central government originally imposed by a foreign conqueror, and destined to break up once again into its component parts when the traditions established by the foreigner will have died away.

I am not concerned for the moment with the political implications of such assertions. Few countries in the world, I venture to say, need as much as India does a patient, sympathetic, and relatively long study before they will disclose their secrets; few countries refuse as firmly as India to be imprisoned within a formula. The very sons of India, when circumstances of upbringing and education oblige them to see India with eyes other than their own, have to make, like Jawaharlal Nehru, the "discovery of India" in manhood, or even in late life. Such a discovery does reveal a basic unity, a common outlook on life, certain concepts of social living, and a general similarity of psychological reactions which entitle us to speak of India as a single entity. But rather, as time goes on, it seems there is emerging in India a physical type which, notwithstanding differences of racial origin, reveals a surprising similarity among people of North and South, of East and West. The body of India may indeed be "multicolored" like the garment of Joseph, but her soul is one. And it is of the soul we have to speak today. Throughout her long and tortuous history, India has been conscious of her soul, conscious of it not only in the hours of her successes but equally in moments of failure, in the hours of her political humiliation and social vicissitude — a soul patient, silent, sensitive, and also willful, resentful of external force, and determined to be always herself.

Nor is it surprising, historically speaking, that India should be conscious of her soul, because her religious and philosophic quest began ages ago, not with the scientific effort to find out the *cause* of things, but to discover the *soul* of things, the individual soul, or the Atman, and the universal soul, the Paramatman. All the later variations of her philosophic quest and her religious passion do not obliterate the fact that the philosophy of India is essentially a philosophy of the soul; all her ascetic effort was for the liberation of the soul; all her mystic ardor, for the union of the individual soul with the Universal Soul. This fact gives not only unity to the people of India but continuity to her history. As she began so she has continued. She was only being true to herself when she called the latest, and in some ways the greatest, of her leaders, Mahatma, "the great soul." And Mahatma Gandhi taught his people to resist the strength of a mighty empire with "soul force," as he called it, to gain their independence by Satyagraha, not by force of arms.

What are the psychological peculiarities of the Indian people which set them on this path of search for the soul of things? Why did the Aryan race which had a different evolution elsewhere — in Greece, in Rome, in the Celtic and Germanic countries — take this particular turn in India? Was it the climate, and the extraordinary profusion of nature in the Indo-Gangetic plain, which, rendering physical labor less easy and less necessary, developed the tendency to reflection? Was it reflection or intuition or imagination which gave them the conviction that "Being" as such must be eternal, if indeed something does exist; that the problem before the philosopher is to explain not the Absolute but the contingent? It is difficult to answer these questions. It may well be that what is ordinarily said to be the result of an intuition is in reality the fruit of rapid subconscious reasonings, coming up to the surface in a flash, *ictu trepidantis oculi*, as St. Augustine says. Again the power of synthesis which generalizes on the basis of many concrete instances is closely allied to the imagination. These intuitions and imaginings act and in their turn are acted upon by the feelings and emotions. The children of Aryavarta were an intensely emotional, imaginative, and intuitive people. Under the rapid flux, the ever changing pageant of the external world, they sensed an absolute unchangeable Reality.

Having reached this point, they set themselves to the task of discovering the nature and attributes of that Reality, the Soul of the Universe. The same spirit of intuitive reflection which led them to postulate a Universal Soul made them sense the permanent reality behind the growing, changing body and the external actions of man, the soul of man. Then, on a day of far-reaching consequence, they reached the conclusion that the individual soul and the Universal Soul were identical, that there was but one sole reality. *Tat tvam asi* — "You are That." *Ekam ēva aditīyam* — "There is but one without a second."

Expressed in this way, it would seem that there is nothing exceptional, nothing specially characteristic of India in this monistic or pantheistic solution of the problem of existence. Many another thinker, unable to reach the height of the conception of a Personal God, infinite and eternal, creator of secondary beings not out of pre-existing material but by the decree of His will, has reached a similar conclusion. And a monistic solution almost inevitably develops, at least among some people, into a crude materialism. The Monism of Hegel has ended in the materialism of Marx. But such a judgment would be wrong about India though India too has her schools of materialism. In the first place it should be remembered that Indian Vedantic thought is not a monism but a nondualism, Advaita: *aditīyam*, "there is no second." It denies the existence neither of the Absolute nor of phenomenal things differentiated from the Absolute, but only of an ultimate and fundamental difference between them. This spiritual monism accepts the presence of matter but gives it only an illusory reality. Furthermore, it takes more literally than we do the statement that we are dreams and shadows. "Dreams are we, visions, shadows strange," says Alice Meynell. Sankaracharya, the greatest champion of Advaita — metaphysician, incomparable dialectician, organizer of the Hindu triumph over Buddhism in the eighth century — even speaks thus:

Though difference be none, I am Thine,
And not Thou O Lord, of me,
Verily the sea is not of the wave
But the wave is of the sea.

If the remorseless logician in Sankara could be brought to say this, be made to speak of the Impersonal Parabrahman as the Lord, how much more the other Acharyas, the great Ramanujam, founder of the School of Vishistadvaita — Advaita with a difference, Father of the theistic Vashnavaite cult; how very much more Madhwa, the founder of the Dualistic or Dvaita School, the only one of the greater Hindu thinkers whose doctrine approximates the doctrine of Creation as we understand it, who did not think that the doctrine of eternal punishment is inconsistent with the goodness of God. These two examples give you some idea of the wide variety of Hindu religious and philosophic schools, one of which, the School of Bhakti or Devotion, closely connected with the Vashnava cult, must momentarily hold our attention.

Since the human soul comes from God and suffers from its involvement in matter, its one effort should be to attain deliverance from the flesh and return to God. The Sanscrit word for "heaven" is *Moksha*, which means "deliverance." There are many different ways of securing such a deliverance and escaping from the cycle of terrestrial births and deaths. They are described in different treatises, but the summary of them found in the favorite devotional scripture of modern India, the Bhagavad Gita, is sufficient for all those seeking to understand this aspect of Hindu thought. There are, first of all, the ways or *Margas* comprising different types of *action*, namely asceticism; or the performance of sacrificial and purificatory ceremonies; of fidelity to Dharma, i.e., the faithful fulfillment of the duties of one's state and condition. But all these actions must be *nishkama karma*, performed in the spirit of total detachment, without desiring any fruit from them. Desire or passion implies attachment to the earth and will mean inevitably a rebirth. Second, there is the way of contemplation or meditation by which the soul comes to the realization of its identity with Brahman. Yogic practices, now often presented as useful types of physical exercise, were originally meant to give complete mastery of the body and its faculties so that the soul might contemplate the Absolute and realize its oneness with that Absolute.

These are difficult and laborious ways of attaining salvation. Is there not a better way still, asks the disciple of Kirshna, in the Bhagavad Gita? Yes, answers the Master who is none other than the Avatar of Vishnu. There is the way of devotion and love when one performs all one's actions out of a motive of pure love for the Lord, and He by His grace alone delivers the soul from the weight of guilt or Karma and grants him deliverance. This cult of Bhakti, which is first enunciated in the Gita, has had a long and varied development in different parts of India, and has inspired some of the noblest expressions of devotion in Indian religious literature. There are those who believe that it has been influenced by the example of Christian communities which have established themselves in several parts of India, notably the West Coast, from the earliest years. This is the opinion of Sir George Grierson, a scholar of unquestioned authority. However this may be, it remains true that the finest utterances of the poets of Bhakti come nearest to the language of Christian mystics. A few quotations will make this clear.

The first will be from Bhagavad Gita itself:

> When you bring to me in adoration a leaf, a flower, a fruit or water, I accept and I receive them as a loving offering. Thus therefore, whatever you do, whatever you eat, whatever you sacrifice, whatever you give and whatever you suffer, O son of Kunti, offer them to me!
>
> Even the most sinful man, if he approaches me in adoration and directs toward me all his worship, must be regarded as good because he has chosen the good way. Soon he will become just and will walk toward eternal happiness. Son of Kunti, proclaim this, he who adores me shall not perish.

The second will be from Tukaram, seventeenth century, the greatest of the Maharashtrian Bhaktas, the chanting of whose hymns fosters the devotion of millions of Maharashtrians today. The first will be a declaration of faith:

> Cursed be that knowledge which makes me one with thee; I love to have precepts from thee and prohibitions.
>
> I am thy servant; thou art my Lord. Let there be still between us such difference of high and low, let this wonderful difference be established, destroy it not.
>
> Water cannot taste itself, nor trees taste their own fruit; the worshipper must be separate, thus alone pleasure arises from distinction (Fraser and Marathe, *Poems of Tukaram*, p. 76).

The next is a passionate cry to Vithoba (Krishna worshiped in Pandarpur):

> A beggar at your door, I stand and I implore
> Give me an alms, O God,
> Love from your loving hands.
> Spare me the bitter task of coming and going with empty hand.
> It is a gift, it is bounty, that Tuka begs,
> Unmerited, unpaid for!

And last from the twentieth century, this perfect piece from Rabindranath Tagore:

> Day after day, O Lord of my life, shall I stand before thee face to face?
>
> With folded hands, O Lord of all the worlds, shall I stand before thee face to face?

> Under thy great sky, in solitude and silence, shall I stand before thee face to face?
>
> In this laborious world of thine, tumultuous with toil and with struggle, shall I stand before thee face to face?
>
> And when my work shall be done in this world, O King of kings, alone and speechless, shall I stand before thee face to face?

Keeping these brief and necessarily simplified historical data as a background, we may proceed to sum up the broad characteristics of Hindu thought and spirituality insofar as they are common to all the schools. That will help us to understand to some extent the soul of India. Speaking broadly we may say that the Indian mind is dominated by the thought of God, God as the source and the end of human existence. From Him we come, and to Him we go. This may not mean exactly what it means to the Christian. But however they may define and understand God, this much is certain — He is conceived as something absolute, universal, formless, changeless, eternal, and, when all things are said, incomprehensible to the human intellect, and inexpressible except by negative terms. To try every possible and conceivable means to know It better and come closer to It — means varying from the highest intellectual and ascetical discipline to the grossest superstition — has been the one unchanging quest of three thousand years of India's history. As Father Broderick says in his life of St. Francis Xavier:

> The most religious land in the world, a land which taught countless millions of men to pray, Chinese and Japanese no less than Hindus. How tawdry and insignificant the brief histories and imperial ambitions of Spain, France, Holland and England appear when set over India's three thousand years of ceaseless passionate search for the eternal and the divine. The gross superstitions and popular idolatory which St. Francis witnessed are not the whole of the story but its least significant part, and all aberrations considered, it seems true of India, as it was of Francis himself, that God is its entire adventure (pp. 326, 327).

If the preoccupation with God and the need to go back to Him in some way is the dominant thought of India, it follows that the objects of an Indian's admiration more than all others will be men who have renounced the ambitions of this world, who have detached themselves and achieved a measure of success in approaching God

The cult of the saint, the holy man, is one of the great passions of the Indian mind. The ruler, the man of science, the man of industry and wealth are respected and admired. But the man of God is loved and worshiped. Thousands of men and women will come from long distances merely to gain one glimpse of a holy man, as millions flocked to see the frail figure of Mahatma Gandhi. There is a Hindu saying that holy idols purify if one worships them and offers sacrifice to them; that holy rivers purify if one bathes in them; but the holy man sanctifies if one looks at him or has a Darshana of him. All success is attributed to the blessing of God and to the blessing of the holy man. It matters little to what religion the holy man belongs, provided he is known as a man of God. How many Hindu students come to the Fathers who teach them and ask for their blessing in moments of importance! How often on being congratulated on some success they answer immediately and almost instinctively, "Your blessing, Father, it was by your blessing."

In order to go back to God, there is no single exclusive way but many ways, or *margas*. I have indicated some of these *margas* already. They are *margas* within the Hindu fold. But the Hindu, particularly the modern Hindu, regards other religions also as acceptable *margas* which the historical and cultural background of each people have developed for themselves and which are therefore more suited to those people. In other words, the Hindu tends to regard religions as we regard schools of spirituality within the Catholic Church. He does believe that the Hindu way has a certain superiority, and now more than ever he would like to see that way accepted by others who are not Hindus by birth. But the fact remains that faith in a clearly defined revelation is not for him a necessary condition of salvation. We see here the consequence of the failure to grasp the essential transcendence of God the Creator, the existence of mysteries in Him, and the need for an authoritative revelation if we are to know anything about His intimate life. This "dogmatic indifference" has, however, made the Hindu an exceptionally tolerant person. Hindu society has in general welcomed the preachers of all religions. Hindu kings from the earliest times protected Christian missionaries and allowed them to preach the Faith. There has been hardly any religious persecution in the strict sense by Hindu rulers. It is typical of Hinduism that if today you go up the great Rock Temple in Trichiopoly opposite St. Joseph's University College, you will find within its precincts Hindus who sell medals of our Lord which they have made. I asked one of them whom they represented. He looked at me in surprise and answered in Tamil, "It is *Hirudayanather*," the Lord of the Sacred Heart.

But while theoretically there is no exclusive way for securing salvation or liberation, there is in practice a device recommended to all: the discipleship of a holy man, his guidance in initiating one to the disciplines that will lead to deliverance. This is the reason why there have been in India at all times holy men who have founded *ashramas* and gathered around themselves disciples whom they initiated to the spiritual life. Respect for the teacher, or *Gurubhakti* as it is called, has always been a characteristic of India. But when the *Guru* is not merely a savant but a saint the respect amounts to worship. As in medieval times in Europe a famous teacher brought to his university students from all countries, so the fame of some holy man brings to his *ashramam* pilgrims and disciples from all walks of life. This often ends in the founding of a new sect or new type of religious activity. A host of names come to mind — the *Tamil Saivites* saints, the *Mahratti Bhaktas* of Vitobha, the *Bengalis* like Chaitanya, Vallabha, Kabit, Ramanand, down to their modern compeers like Ramakriohna, Sai Baba, Aurobindo Ghose, and Ramana Maharshi of Tiruvannamalai. It is noteworthy that some of them were low-caste people, even Untouchables. The obstinate prejudices of caste do not operate when dealing with holy men. They are *jivanmuktis*, souls that have secured a liberation even in this life, as we might say "souls confirmed in grace." They are above sex, caste, religion.

As we have seen, liberation means freedom from the trammels of the flesh and from the necessity of birth in the material world. Now, birth and caste, along with the rigid Hindu social system, go together. Whatever the origin of caste, the doctrine of Metempsychosis or reincarnation in conditions predetermined by the merits and faults of the previous life made caste a religious institution, the expression of a divinely instituted social order. Fidelity to the prescriptions of caste, the faithful fulfillment of the duties enjoined by the state of life which birth and caste give to a man constitute *Dharma* in the broadest sense. *Dharma* is cognate with the Latin word *dare*, "*to give*"; it means that which is given, a code of conduct imposed from above and binding by divine law insofar as we can speak of divine law in the Vedantic system. These duties were formulated by the lawgiver Manu, and his system, the *Manava Dharma Shastra*, has ruled Hindu society for two thousand years. The Neo-Hindu reformers who are trying to dethrone Manu and who declare that caste is an extraneous accretion which does not affect the substance of Hinduism do not probably realize how revolutionary their ideas are, and how surely they are laying the ax to the roots of traditional Hinduism.

The institution of caste and an extraordinary strength of family attachment go together. They constitute one of the distinctive characteristics of Indian civilization and therefore one of the typical manifestations of the Indian soul. This is undoubtedly a case of reciprocal causality. The strength of family attachment must have had much to do with the evolution of the institution of caste, and caste in its turn maintains the strength and purity of family life. The sense of blood relationship is very highly developed in India. It has led to the emergence of the joint family system in which the property of a family is neither divided and distributed nor transmitted to the elder son, but remains family property owned by all the brothers and their children living together under the same roof under the rule of the eldest member of the family. The children of brothers and sisters call themselves brothers and sisters. There is no word in Indian languages for cousins. One has to question and find out if someone introduced as a brother is really a brother or a cousin. The duty of providing for not only one's own children but for a large family circle is accepted by all Indians who live in a joint family. They find it difficult to understand the opposition to "nepotism and favoritism" in New India with its inculcation of civic virtues. They do not see why what was a virtue in the traditional society should suddenly become a crime in the new set-up!

There is no doubt that the strength of family loyalties is a characteristic of Asian civilization as a whole. It may explain the political weakness of Asia in the past, because for Asians the ideal of social development did not go along lines of national unity and uniformity as for the inheritors of the Graeco-Roman tradition, but along the line of family and community solidarity. It developed dynastic loyalties but not patriotism in the European sense. In India, the strong social instinct of the people found expression in communal and not civic life. And this has a close connection with the religious inspiration of Asian and in particular Indian civilization. Caste is an excellent example of the integration of family and religion.

Another deep-seated instinct of the Indian soul flowing from the notion of Karma and Dharma is the sense of retribution; the conviction that actions cannot be isolated but that they draw an inevitable consequence of good or bad; that for all human actions there is ultimate justice in this life or in a future birth. The only way of escaping the consequences of one's action is to perform disinterested action, *nishkama karma*. It is clear that this somewhat impersonal *nishkama karma* is very different from the pure love, *amor purus*, of the Christian mystic. At the same time we must recognize that psychologically the habit of disinterested action will facilitate acts of disinterested love.

It is easy to prolong this list of characteristics but let us conclude by noting the Indian attitude to animals and to life in general. The pantheistic background of Indian thought inspires the sentiment of the sacredness of all life. Here again there may be an element of rationalizing and of reciprocal causality. The sensitive, imaginative Indian mind has a great natural sense of pity, of Karunai, the pity which led Prince Gautama to meditate on the cause of suffering and along the road to final Enlightenment, Bodhi. Pity and the sense of the sacredness of life have acted and reacted upon each other and developed the doctrine of Ahimsa, nonviolence, one of the outstanding contributions of India to the thought of the world, a moral and social force of immense power from the time of

Asoka to that of Mahatma Gandhi. It has also led to that strange characteristically Indian familiarity between man and beast which endows animals with human feelings and instincts, and in the literature of fable and allegory — a genus very characteristic of India — makes them talk and act like humans. You will remember the fables of Pilpay or Bidpay, whose correct Indian name was Vidyapati, fables which have found their way into many European collections including those of La Fontaine. Again this sense of the oneness of the pervading spirit has led many sensitive Indian poets of all ages to fuse together and present as one moving unity, as the expression of one basic life, the world of men and women, of bird and beast, of flower and tree, of wind and water. In all this there is a degree of what may be called poetic truth which everyone can appreciate and take delight in. But in India it has metaphysical undertones which are impossible to mistake, undertones heard also in certain modern English poets like Wordsworth and Thomas Hardy.

And yet, strangely and paradoxically, as so often happens in India, this sense of pity and the sacredness of life exists side by side with an apparent indifference, an apparent callousness to human suffering, and even cruelty to animals which have shocked foreign observers. What is the cause of this? I believe it is due to the other doctrine of the ascetical value of suffering, to the belief in Karma and the divinely ordained social system or Dharma, by which each man must endure the lot that is his. This has prevented among a kindly people the growth of organized works of charity and social benevolence such as the religious orders have fostered in Europe. And even when there is charity it is curiously impersonal without the warmth of love, as when a Brahmin widow, from a sense of penance or desire to gain merit, waits with a pot of cold water along a public road on a sultry day and will pour it into the half-closed palms of the pedestrian without a word and without even a straight look at him.

These broad philosophical and psychological attitudes had developed and become part of the Hindu mind before the modern impact of Western and Christian ideas on India which one hundred fifty years of Western political domination, Western education, and missionary activity have brought about. These have led to a far-reaching revolution in India which has still not worked itself out. It will take a century, perhaps many centuries, before a full synthesis of the old and the new exteriorly and interiorly, in body and mind, will fully emerge. The intellectual history of India has ever been of this type: readiness to accept ideas from wherever they may come, to brood over them through long years, to choose, to assimilate, or simply to add them on as the mood takes her; but always after putting on each of these acquisitions some peculiar stamp of her own, so that a generation later she comes to believe that it was part of her inheritance from the earliest times! So at the present moment it is possible to note only a few points which have resulted from the impact of Christian ideas.

The influence of Christianity and to a lesser extent the influence of Islam at an earlier period have certainly given an impetus to the Bhakti cults and a specially increasing importance to the worship of the Avatars of Vishnu — Krishna and Rama. Already the Ramayana of Tulsidas, the Bible of a hundred million people, had made this cult the most powerful in northern India. In more recent years the cult of Krishna and the popularity of the Bhagavad Gita have had an ever widening vogue, replacing, with the warmth of personal devotion, the cult of the impersonal Brahman typical of classical Hinduism. Even more than this, in some reformed groups, like the Brahmo Samajists, the influence of Christianity is seen in their unequivocal theism and total opposition to idolatry and even abandonment of the doctrine of reincarnation. At the same time there has been an extraordinary movement for social reform, of opposition to caste and untouchability, to the age-long hardships imposed upon women; a new sense of social responsibility in regard to the poor and the suffering, the sick and the abandoned. There is high appreciation of the Gospels and a great admiration and love for the person of Jesus. This does not amount, however, to a recognition of His claim to a unique Sonship of God and the need to adhere to Him by sacramental Baptism. It is common enough to hear the distinction between "the religion of Jesus" and "the religion of the Church."

All these instances of Christian influence may be discerned and exemplified in the teaching and person of Mahatma Gandhi. He is typical of the old and the new, a Vaishnaya Hindu rooted in the thought of God, conservative to the point of believing in caste — the Varnasharama Dharma — and even the sacredness of the cow, ascetical, given to the cult of fasting and prayer; and yet a reformer whose wrath against the curse of untouchability and the pride of caste, against the oppression of woman and cruelty to the widow, was like a consuming fire; a Hindu, yet one who never or hardly ever worshiped in a temple; a lover of the Gospel and of the Person of Jesus whose Sermon on the Mount was one of his favorite spiritual readings and inspired in part his doctrine of passive resistance. More than all these there is in Mahatma Gandhi a new attitude toward suffering, a tenderness and pity for sufferers, a sense of the value of suffering not only as means of personal purification but as expiation for the crimes of others; in a word, an understanding of the mystery of the Cross. Indeed the Protestant hymn "When I Behold the Wondrous Cross" was one of his favorites. It is safe to say that on suffering Mahatma Gandhi has spoken in accents which had never been heard before among men of his faith.

Since we have been speaking of the impact of Christianity, and since there are so many denominations of Christians who have done missionary work in India, which of these denominations most attract the Hindu mind? Or better still, what is its attitude toward Catholicism and Protestantism? Do Indians see the difference between them; have they preferences for one or the other? It must be confessed that, being somewhat indifferent to varieties and differences of belief among themselves, to a large extent they tend not to make too much of a distinction between Protestant and Catholic. They look upon all as "Christians" with minor differences among themselves. But when they come to look more closely and see that the divergences are not superficial, they can judge for themselves with shrewdness.

They admire in Protestants precisely the liberal spirit which permits a great variety of beliefs. They admire their prominence and success in works of education and social beneficence, and indeed Protestants were active in education and medical work earlier than Catholics. Moreover, the influence of English literature and the prestige of the English-speaking world in economics, in industry, in applied science attracted them to Protestant culture. They were confirmed in this attraction by the widespread prejudices against the Church, her alleged corruption, obscurantism, and intolerance which English Protestant literature and textbooks of history commonly disseminate.

On the other hand, there is much in the Catholic faith and practice which appeals to them with great force because it resembles in so many ways their own traditions and customs. They admire the ideal of asceticism and renunciation in Catholic monasticism. They understand and desire the use of ceremonies, of sacramental symbolism in worship, the use of external helps like pictures and statues, processions and pilgrimages. Above all they admire and feel at home in the Catholic cult of the saints and of the Blessed Virgin. Without saints and the Blessed Virgin, without ceremonies and external liturgy, Protestantism seems to them to be a cold and purely rational religion. There are shrines to saints and to the Blessed Virgin in India. Two famous shrines of our Lady are those of Velangany on the east coast near Negapatam and in Bandra near Bombay. Hindus flock to these shrines in large numbers; judging only by figures, they are more numerous than the Catholics.

By way of conclusion, if I am asked, not indeed to sum up all the attributes of the soul of India — that would be an impossible task — but to indicate its distinctive feature, I would say that it consists in a certain tension of soul caused by the attraction of opposite ideals, and, less healthy, the contradiction between opposite instincts; a tension and a contradiction which she has not been able to resolve. We thus have the concept of God as Paratman and God as Ishvara, the way of knowledge and the way of love; opposition between the sense of the unity of all things, and so of the equality of all men, and a most rigid and exclusive social organization; opposition already noted between pity and respect for life and an apparent callousness toward suffering; opposition between the ideal of detachment and the habit of purposeful action which prompts at times an astonishing egoism that insists nothing is done for nothing and it is right to do a good turn with the hope that it will inspire a favor in return. Again there is the widest doctrinal tolerance with great social intolerance; a real openness of mind and readiness to welcome new ideas and a narrowness and touchiness which resent any statement of indebtedness to other people or other religions in the matter of doctrine and religious practices. This affects the attitude to even scientific inventions and discoveries and leads to fantastic claims that the ancient Indians knew how to construct airplanes and were familiar with the radio and the wireless. There is opposition between a high spirituality and the tolerance of the crudest superstitions and forms of worship; firm belief in Revelation and Tradition, Sruti and Smritc, and an almost anarchic freedom of speculation.

We must add to these age-long oppositions the tension caused by the impact of the modern world on the older culture of India, the new social upsurges, the clash between the ideal of caste and community and the new ideal of nation and state. These contradictions have weakened India materially and brought much misery to her people. But they have kept alive the energy of her spirit and the keenness of her intellect because she has tried continually to find a principle of unity which will enable her to integrate all these elements in a unified culture just as she is trying to integrate her many races and languages into a single nation. But in the sphere of ideas, unity is not possible without some necessary sacrifices. Heaven and earth can be reconciled. But truth and untruth, good and evil, cannot be reconciled.

To the oppositions already indicated it is necessary to add yet another: love of Jesus Christ and refusal to recognize His visage in the lineaments of His Church, like Him wounded and bleeding and crucified again and again; like Him, unwearied in her ministrations, preaching, comforting, healing; like Him humble yet speaking with authority, patient, submissive, yet fearless and heroic. India has seen her, heard her voice, and sometimes engaged in dialogue with her. But she does not recognize in her Him whose Mystical Body she is. Like the disciples of Emmaus who walked with Him without recognizing Him, her vision is clouded. We the children of this much loved motherland of ours who know and love Christ in Himself and in His Church can never give up the hope and prayer that this unfinished dialogue of hers with the Church may end in recognition; that she may see in Him and His Church the principle of unity which alone reconciles opposites, earth and heaven, time and eternity, humanity and divinity, death and life; that after that glad recognition we may all sit together for the breaking of Bread, foretaste of the eternal banquet which will be the fulfillment of the beatitude which is peculiarly India's: "Blessed are they that hunger and thirst for justice, for they shall be satisfied."

LATIN AMERICA

BY SIR JAMES BRURON SUBIABRE . . . *Born, Chile, February 7, 1914; educated by the Brothers of the Christian Schools; followed higher commercial school; manager of a wine-culture plant; director of Corporacion Vitivinicola De Chile; president of Archdiocesan Catholic Action and vice-president of National Catholic Action; founder of Catholic Group of the Mountains of Valparaiso; ex-president, Catholic Youth of Valparaiso; ex-president, National Conference of Trade and Industry; commander of Order of St. Gregory the Great; commander of Order of the French Vinestalk; member of Third Order of St. Francis; author of* Manual Del Dirigente De Catholic Action

---

Latin America still remains the unknown and very often unappreciated "New World." Europe and the rest of the world show great ignorance in this respect and an appalling mixture of partial and ambiguous knowledge.

An American boy attending a secondary school knows much more about the history of Europe, her political and cultural evolution, than most European adults know about the rich history of South America. As far as geography is concerned, some public European offices situate Santiago of Chile in Mexico or Nicaragua or Argentina.

But this ignorance is much more serious in respect to the manners and customs, culture and soul of so-called Latin America, this continent which under many aspects has great hopes of a tremendous future. European people have some recollection of revolutions of purely Indian people and of unstable governments, but they forget the main thing: the very life of these people, which took its source in the Indian peninsula and became deeper by the enrichments of European art and culture, as it still does. The spirit of Christ rules amid all these elements, strengthens them, enlightens them, although it is not yet fully lived and assimilated.

It is not merely interesting, it is also necessary to speak about the soul of Latin America. When they have true mutual knowledge the people of the world will no longer ignore or caricature each other, but they will understand, appreciate, and love each other. To understand Latin Americans it is necessary to know and understand the extension and variety of the land they live in, their various origins, their social, economic, and religious achievements, some of which are of the pre-Columbian period. It is also indispensable to know their past and present dynamics, their progress, their capabilities, and their various arts. The soul reveals itself in deeds, attitudes are shown in actual life, especially in Latin America, where like in Spain the soul of the people is skin-deep and their feelings are betrayed in gestures and in looks.

If Columbus, when he reached the little island of Guanahani, has seen the huge territory of the New World, he would not have believed his own eyes. Nor might the Spanish and Portuguese have been so enthusiastic, if they had seen the fields, the mountains, the streams, the sea, and the deserts. Later, in the course of action, it was only by the strength of their souls that these men could master the superhuman difficulties of discovery and conquest. The qualities of soul of the natives awaiting the conquerors at the doors of Tiahuanaco, Cuzco, Tectihuacan, or in Araocania, were better preserved than their blood in this great mixture of people that followed the conquest.

It is much easier to make a study of a nation having strictly limited and well-defined frontiers, than to get an intimate knowledge of populations living far away from the nearest town, in countries where roads 700 miles long are most common. The whole of Europe could be included two and one-half times in Latin America. Chile is 2600 miles long, which is equal to the distance from Oslo to the center of French Africa. In a single country, almost in one province, it is possible to find all the climates of the world, from ski runs to deserts and pleasant seashores. The whole stretch can be covered in a few hours.

Leaving out the United States and Canada, and considering the whole area between the Rio Bravo and the Antarctic Circle, Latin America embraces twenty independent nations, not including the white territories of the Antarctic belonging to Chile and Argentina. The above delimited area covers about 15½ million square miles, with a population of 180 million inhabitants. In 1920, this population was 84 million, less than half of what it is today. This same phenomenon did not occur during this century in any other region, within such a short time, or affecting such a great number of people. The yearly rate of increase in Latin America exceeds by far the figures of any other region in the world.

Besides the geographical extension, other aspects must be considered, namely the human capital represented by this increase of population, its influence on progress, the increased returns obtained by the solution of various problems concerning sanitation, town administration, political and ecclesiastical life, and, above all, food distribution, dwellings, and education.

Latin America is a huge cradle, full of new lives whose features cannot yet be outlined. Who could predict what will become of these youngsters during the next forty years? If the mortality rate continues to decrease and the birth rate maintains its present figures, it may be reckoned that the population will one day reach the 400 million mark.

In spite of the marvelous panoramas of a most picturesque country, and its extraordinary fecundity, grave problems arise for the government, educators, intellectuals, and leaders. How can the thirst for culture, orientation, and true formation be satisfied? How can a dignified and human level of life be achieved to the increasing number of families?

How will it be possible to give the people and the nations a philosophy based on historical experience and actual life which will lead them toward a destiny ever more human and dignified? Not only for the benefit of individual countries, but for the whole of humanity, a way should soon be found to prevent the generations that live so fast from fighting against each other, or starting revolutions for the sake of short-lived and destructive illusions.

Let us consider what characterizes most of Latin America. Which way must be followed? What is to be done in a practical way? Which are the abstract principles that could support and improve human values?

The standard of life of the workmen ought to be improved. Indians must be protected and promoted. The social and legal structure must be improved. The sources of production, food, clothing, habitation, education, and instruction must be developed. Health must be protected. Everybody agrees upon all this, but the question is: How will it be possible to reach this ideal? We shall consider later on the part to be played by Christian principles in reaching the aim fixed by men.

Latin America has produced eminent men who were conspicuous in various spheres such as science, art, and literature. Some before and others after the emancipation of the country predicted in their writings the future of the land and of the people. We may also mention painters, musicians, sculptors, university professors who can be compared with their colleagues of the Old World; missionaries who baptized, instructed, understood, and defended the natives and started the first social redemption of the poorer populations. But the great mass of people is composed of 59 million illiterates over 15 years of age. These people live between the Cordillera, in the Pampas, on the endless coasts, on the mountains, in the woods. This overwhelming majority represents 90 per cent in Haiti, 54 per cent in Mexico, 51 per cent in Brazil, 44 per cent in Chile, 51 per cent in Colombia, 14 per cent in Uruguay.

A number of consequences result from these figures, but we must also take into account another mass composed of children who go to school but do not terminate their studies. The pupils who reach the end of the primary grades represent only 6 per cent. The problem is the same for the other degrees of studies as well as for the universities.

The framework must be changed more or less rapidly, according to the countries. Great efforts are made privately as well as officially to increase the level of general education in Latin America. Among other countries, good examples are given to this effect by Mexico and Colombia, and radio is used for education purposes. The top priority must be given to primary education, and everybody must be concerned with the basic formation of the people.

The laity and the clergy have a big part to play, because it would be impossible for the State to effect it alone. The State has appealed to the Catholic Church and she has given extensive co-operation, as much in the towns as all over the country. "To govern is to teach" is the motto of one South American government, and several government schemes are much concerned with the fundamental requirements of education. In Latin America, each parish is a small or large center of primary or secondary schools. According to the idea expressed by Pope Pius XI: "It is no use to build a church, if a school cannot be found close to it." The Church is not only a supernatural but a natural teacher.

Today the soul of Latin America is very conscious of its duty to take the attitude of a teacher. The responsibilities in this respect are shared by professional teachers, families, syndicates, social leaders, soldiers, and policemen. It is not only the number of the population but its culture that must be increased.

Besides, this effort would be false, if one would not take into account three factors of culture to be found among the illiterates, which have been acquired by the maturity of their minds and their behavior in life. For education purposes, the native values must be taken into consideration, although they are not always easy to distinguish; they appear however almost anywhere in the ideas of the common people, in their songs, food, dances, and even in their religion, where some heathen rites can be found.

This educational and intellectual duty is also connected with other and deeper problems. The slow cultural development of the people prevents them from taking judicious advantage of technical progress. People who ignore the use of a toothbrush make a rush on the radio. They use a tractor without being able to manage an old-style plow. They want to get a refrigerator, but they cannot use a bathroom.

It must not be thought that this revolutionary fashion of progressing in cultural maturation is of no importance. If technical progress is to be at the service of man, it is important that the fruits of it should not give man, as from his childhood, a false idea concerning true appreciation of human values. This is possibly the most difficult point to solve for anyone who wants to make immediate use of progress while taking care not to spoil by inconsidered haste the whole of his human characters. To more material improvements of the facilities of life and better technical results must correspond a larger spiritual value, a broader vision of human destinies, a better understanding of the greatness of the human creature who stands much higher than his own creations. The terrifying fact is that today maturation does not wait, and while man may be deprived of an inner culture, he is covered from the outside by all sorts of material advantages and surpassed by events. It is a heavy and crushing pace for a man whose soul has not enough fortitude to stand against it and to master it from the inside. But on the other hand, it is a splendid instrument for the mastery of man over material things, if his spirit is stronger than external progress.

The duty to teach a man, or in some way to make a man, is a task which has been undertaken in all the countries of Latin America, generally with some hesitation, but in a decisive and enlightened way, by the more intellectual organizations.

Besides, I would like to state that I am not a pessimist and that I am not placing Latin America in a situation inferior to the other regions of the world. If a serious comparison could be made of the past, as well as of the present, it would certainly place us in a good position; but the soul of Latin America, being desirous of improving itself, is more interested in future opportunities and obligations than in mere reflection on the past. Whatever the greatness of the work achieved since the schools for Indians, the Franciscan, Jesuit, Dominican, and Augustinian establishments, the universities of Santo Domingo and Nueva Espana, which have since been imitated in all America; and despite the emancipation, the educational work of the republics, and the present primary and secondary schools, technical preparation in the universities and specialized institutes, the highest disciplines of most renowned faculties in the universities — all this, I repeat, although it is great and admirable, is but small progress in the face of what remains to be done according to our desires.

The Latin American people are very anxious to increase their standard of living in all its aspects, namely with regard to lodging, food, and conditions of work.

To make a detailed analysis of this program would involve a preliminary study of economic geography, because a great variety of ways of life is to be found in a country as large and diverse as South America. In the southern part of Chile and Argentina there is snow and wind like in Belgium or Germany, while in the northern part of these same countries the climate is similar to western French Africa. Why talk about differences between one country and another? The altitude above sea level of certain towns in Bolivia is higher than many peaks in the Alps, and yet Bolivia has large fields of caco, forests, and tropical climate. Colombia is a three-level country. Brazil is a continent by itself and its government has to deal with extremely remote regions.

So the problems of the South, with regard to lodging, are not the same as in the Equator, nor are the questions concerning food and regulations of work; but whatever the differences, the same main objective is that in his respective climate, with his local customs, in snow or in heat, the man, his family, and his children may be provided with food, lodging, and work in proportion to his dignity.

When Padre Las Casas, at the beginning of the conquest, took up the defense of the Indians, few people shared his concern, but increasing interest was shown later in protecting the humble workman against injustice and misery. This movement started with the suppression of slavery and developed steadily into modern labor legislation.

Latin America is still mainly agricultural. The agricultural population reaches 80 per cent in Haiti, as against 30 per cent in Chile and Uruguay. The average percentage for the whole working population of Latin America is 50.7 per cent in respect to agriculture. It is not necessary to stress the influence that this proportion of agricultural population has on the social, cultural, economic, and political character of a nation. The advantages and disadvantages of an agricultural majority have already been examined many times, but when we are considering the improvement of the living standard of the working classes, we must first of all consider the local problems of agriculture in the countries of Latin America. During the last International Congress of Country Life in Santiago, Chile, in 1957, it was made clear that the government as well as individuals was very much interested in increasing productivity in the agricultural industry, reducing the cost and increasing the quality of food and raw material, raising considerably the standard of living of farm workers, preparing a rational and logical emigration plan proportionate to the degree of mechanization reached in agriculture and the development of secondary and technical training.

The agricultural aspect of the country is also reflected in the soul of the people, even in the industrial parts of the country. Amid the machinery and industrial and technical progress, the Latin-American workman cannot get rid of his peasant look. The *Huaso*, the *Gaucho*, the *Charro* are noticed everywhere in the most modern towns and factories. Nature is stronger in the soul of the people than it is in technical achievement.

Besides its 50.7 per cent in agricultural work, Latin America has 18.4 per cent in manufacturing and construction, 27.6 in general services, 1 per cent in the mines, and 2.4 per cent in other activities.

These percentages are not parallel with the figures of economic progress nor equal to the importance the governments have attributed to industry in opposition to agriculture, nor to the cost of administration services which are out of proportion with the economical results. Latin America has too high an opinion of her industries and mines, although they are no doubt important and sometimes impressive. The land is and will remain the big reserve; people who eat well, are well clad, and have enough leisure want further progress. Besides, forces are at hand to assure economic and political development.

In the readjustment of the conditions of life and work of the active population of Latin America, many other factors had to be taken into account, among them the syndical organizations. Some have a merely partisan character; others are purely economic and organized by leaders, sometimes really heroic, who claim higher salaries by putting the ever increasing weight of labor in one scale of the balance of social equilibrium.

But they are not ripe yet for syndicalism. Too many political dictators are to be found among others having genuine syndicalist objectives. Governments occasionally use the syndicate as a political weapon. Some foreign influences have no other object than to create trouble.

True syndicalism will be reached as soon as the work itself has been dignified and the culture of the labor classes developed. Examples of this can already be found in various countries of Latin America, especially where syndicalist liberty exists.

Trying to find the same fundamental aims by other ways and means, employers associations have arisen and still arise in Latin America. Their object is not limited to the economical interests of their own industries, but they aim to create a fairer, more dignified, and efficient labor movement. They take the human rather than the merely technical or financial point of view. Have these efforts been effective as yet in the management of these enterprises and toward a proper orientation between capital and labor? Most probably not. But these efforts have the advantage of youth and strength and the current tendency toward new economic structures works in their favor. These structures will become Marxist, unless they are outbalanced by others having broader views and making stronger efforts to discover and impose more natural and human forms of labor and better social relations.

The Latin American soul is troubled by three different attitudes:

1. It would defend itself by trying to maintain all the present structures.
2. It seeks to penetrate everywhere and pretend to impose the

material Marxist doctrine by placing man at the service of the organization.

3. Conscious of the present evils, it prefers not to reject everything from the past, nor to forget the future, but it seeks a new structure beneficial to all.

We have now reached the third consideration. From Nuova Espana up to the western point of Chile, where Don Fernando de Magellan saw the junction of the two oceans, and all along the projecting bust of Brazil and the straighter outlines of the Pacific coast, with the graceful necklace of the Antilles Islands, Latin America awoke at the steps of the Spanish and Portuguese conquerors and was ready to accept Western civilization.

The American people who did not disown the features resulting from the blood which came from Europe and pre-Columbian America, despite the distances and differences, formed an administrative unity inspired by the fundamental principles of the mother countries. The same language, religion, customs were brought from the Peninsula and, although different, these people began to resemble each other, as parents issued from a common stock resemble each other, although they are different.

Nevertheless, Latin America is an archipelago and, as someone has said, the various islands which compose it are not separated by water, but by deserts, mountains, forests, competition, incomprehension, or they are isolated because they had no time to consider each other while they were paying too much attention to Europe.

The American emancipation, with its wars, revolutions, and vicissitudes, occasioned the formation of new republics with an experience acquired from two empires, but with very little republican maturity; with good organization in some parts, but revolutions in others. All this mixture of historical events, added to the jealousy of foreign powers toward Spain, made Latin America an archipelago for a very long time. The big joint actions, shared by many people and undertaken in favor of liberty, in the case of Bolivar for instance, were unfortunately kept in the background by other more local and immediate events.

Latin America forms a kind of unity. Yet all the events that have contributed to its present form should have been directed to a common goal. It is easier to govern toward unity than toward division. Unfortunately, for a long time to come, the best efforts toward co-ordination and understanding will be lost. People have taken the habit of preferring to work harder, to make the great efforts required by the separation, rather than to join in a logical way efforts undertaken for the common welfare.

It is not that the countries of Latin America have been careless in their endeavors to reach a better understanding and a wider union among themselves. Rather they have not been firm enough or they have had no real chance to achieve their objective. In 1826, Bolivar convened in Panama the first Congress that today we would call Latin American. Two years before, Bolivar wrote from Lima in a letter of invitation addressed to the chiefs of the American States:

> . . . The time has now come, when the interests and relations which unite the American republics should have a fundamental basis in order to perpetuate if possible the duration of these governments.

On this occasion, the formation of a federated army and a fleet for both oceans was allowed, but the resolution remained on paper. San Martin and Bolivar stated at Guayaquil that Latin America was still in the chrysalis stage, and we ourselves must now admit that the metamorphosis is not yet complete. This is because the Latin-American soul is forever struggling to assure its liberty on several fronts. Co-operation and understanding would be possible if all the rulers would give it the same direction, and agree upon the terms for right, human person, dignity, common welfare, authority, and liberty.

Latin America is doing now what others have done for many years, these who have taken part in the struggle for the fundamental liberties of man. The republican or legislative, judicial, and executive powers now maintain themselves sovereign and independent. The law is respected and justice is done. The human person is considered. Universities are free and therefore deserve the name of university. Where this is true, it serves as an example to all who still pursue the fight for progress in their own country.

At the bottom of this deep human problem there is a question of public interest in culture in the midst of misery. When great masses of people live in poverty and a demagogue offers them better conditions of life, liberty is soon reached, because it was only their misery that prevented them from enjoying liberty before.

When college and even clerical education is restricted or badly orientated, when ethics is forgotten and morality becomes merely utilitarian, people let themselves be guided by profit, whatever is available, unless they are proud enough to say with O'Higgins, "Rather live with honor or die with glory."

When national or international commercial interests are regulated by legal or de facto governments, and preference is given to whatever is the most corrupt or venal, it is difficult to be concerned with high principles of liberty and law.

The Latin-American soul is no doubt conscious of its duty. Continental solidarity is often promoted by the press, radio, and various tribunes, and this should help to foster a regime based on respect for the human person and the common welfare.

Latin America is a vast orchard, a rich mine, a huge hydroelectric plant, a tremendous reserve of raw material. Wheat, maize, potatoes, wine, vegetable, oils, meat. What cannot be found in America? The problem is to use it according to the harmonious plans of its Creator.

If the producers of wheat knew that by collecting their crops they were giving some of it to the people who send them sugar; if the growers of coffee and rubber knew that other people were busy extracting copper and coal for them; if the wine was singing in the casks for those who herd flocks in other continents; if the syndicate, the banks, the parliaments would stress in plain American language whatever is legitimately national, then the soul of Latin America would be satisfied because it would be striving in accordance with the order given by Providence.

Let us consider further features of the American soul with its Indian, Latin, Iberian, Negro, French influences.

The worst method for discovering America would be to apply an exclusive name like Native, Spanish, Latin, or other origin to it.

The newborn child will show in his features, in his blood, in his gestures, unmistakable proof of the origin of his ancestors. He will be completely identified. In order to judge him, it will be advisable to know his origins, but it will still be this child and not another, with his own characteristics and peculiarities. America in her full development also wants to be what she really is, and not surrounded by a crowd of relations who resemble her physically and wish to impose a certain way of living upon her.

It is important that the leaders benefit by all the experiences had abroad. It must be noted, however, that an adaptation should be made to the typically American milieu and to the experience of the original inhabitants. The structure, the organs, even the styles receive an American adaptation which brings them into conformity with the life of the population and frees them from a strong foreign taste that would not be acceptable here. When this process of adaptation is terminated, and when the most adequate structures will have been found to build and foster a truly human community, the future will appear much more promising than the past.

The middle class takes a big part in this evolution and adaptation. Formerly, two orders of people existed: the leading class at the top, having power and money, and the laborers at the bottom; but between these two extremes there was no middle class to compensate such a big difference. All countries did not resent to the same extent the weight of these two extremes in their social equilibrium.

But now another factor presents itself in the social picture. University students belong increasingly more to the middle classes, and in consequence there is a substantial increase of middle-class men in the various professions. What is more, the leading class has gradually abandoned managerial work, giving a further increased importance to the middle class. Although this fact does not appear with the same frequency everywhere, it constitutes one of the most important factors determining the features of the American people today. The drive shaft has been shifted, more by evolution than revolution, toward the center of the social collectivity.

As a result, an increased importance has been added to the formation given by the university to those who almost unexpectedly are vested with responsibilities of management and direction.

For the time being, the university, the *Alma Mater*, so precious to the culture of the people, in spite of her brilliant career, fostered in Latin America by the Catholic Church, and open to all disciplines, is not provided for in accordance with her needs, and does not enjoy the liberty required by her irreplaceable work.

The official State university, together with the free universities, Catholic or not, are now facing the greatest responsibilities of their history. They are entrusted with the formation of professionals, technicians, to cope with the needs of the moment, but they must at the same time keep their character of universities and concentrate upon the complete formation of man with regard to universal values, and to prevent deformation by excess of specialization. This specialization is urgently required in a world which must build itself almost all over again, but the formation given at the university must be honest and cultural to humanize the world.

Latin America could achieve unexpected economical and technical progress, but she must avoid the error of looking at man as just one more piece of machinery.

The great problem of humanism facing our people, as well as all Western culture, is man's loss of personality and the necessity for working hard to restore his human character. In Latin America this job takes on certain aspects peculiar to a continent which is in full cultural evolution. We must take advantage of our traditional Christian culture and of the special spiritual and psychological values constituted by our primitive people and by our black inhabitants.

If this renewal of humanism is not soon effected, Communism will be best qualified to play the part of savior.

The complexity of contemporary life claims formulas which include the whole man, or which give at least a complete explanation of his existence. Communism strives to give this explanation on a material basis. Marxist groups include persons of great human and intellectual value who are very active in their respective milieu, especially in the universities, syndicates, artistic groups, etc. Besides the peculiar meaning of Marxism, its introduction in Latin America reveals the latent desire of the people to seek new ways to guide their lives. Consciously or unconsciously, they seek a new world without knowing exactly which is the best way to make it more human.

The new world, according to Don Alonzo de Ercilla and Zuniga in the *Araucania*, "is so great, proud, insolent, and bellicose. It was never ruled by a King nor submitted to foreign commandment."

In the long run, it is Christian baptism which is recognized as having rendered Latin America more human. Christianity may or may not have been fruitful for certain individual Americans, but for the mass of the people it is a seed which still continues to grow and bear fruit. And supposing it did not fructify really and decisively, no one of the Mayas, Aztecs, Incas, or the Patagons, or people of the Amazon and the Orenoc, could be expected to understand a discovery made in the name of the Cross. A civilization which would not dignify men, nor save them for eternity by humanizing them, would not be completely justified. It is the difference between the Cross and the sword and a terrible historical and supernatural responsibility of American Christianity.

From the time the first priests came to America up to the present day; from the time of the strict Indian patronage up to the present republics with or without a regime of separation of Church and State; from the time Our Lady of Guadalupe came to America to cover her with her mantle and her seal up to the present fervent popular manifestations of faith in hundreds of shrines; from the time the first colleges and schools were founded by the Franciscans, Dominicans, Augustinians, and Jesuits up to the several hundred years old universities of Central America, Mexico, and South America; from the foundation of the first hospitals and asylums up to the modern organization for the re-education of the mentally diseased, the rehabilitation of the fallen, the humanizing of prison life; from the time the first efforts were made to humanize and protect the Indians and liberate them from covetousness up to the

Christian inspiration visible in today's legislation of the republics; from the time of the good-natured Christianity of the sixteenth century up to the deep and fruitful efforts made by the apostolate of the laity; from the time of the discovery, the conquest, emancipation, and sovereignty — all this while Catholicism was and is the most permanent support, the backbone visible or invisible, the longest lasting and the best encouragement that was given to the people of Latin America. With her own errors, defects, and human miseries, but always firm, present, and alive with the special character of her divine origin, the Church was really the bosom from which Latin America took her life and development and upon which she will flourish.

But the mission of the Church is far from terminated. Catholicism in Latin America is exceedingly individual and queer, especially in the native and black population where it is mixed with superstition, and in the superior social classes where religion has become a veneer or a convention. What may have been concealed before is more noticeable today because social maturity requires greater preciseness in its attitudes and clearness in its definitions. Half measures no longer suffice when the surroundings require more than mediocrity.

In spite of inevitable loss from diffusion, the Catholic religion is much more intensively practiced today, and people are making sincere efforts to face their responsibilities, both temporal and eternal.

Among the features of a Christianity which does not content itself with past grandeur, we may notice a lively Christian community taking part in the liturgy and the apostolate; religion entering into daily work and into university and family life; intelligence and courage displayed in the big historical moments of the nations; real saintliness in the cloisters, in the parishes, in the institutes, in the great masses of laymen. Multitudes in various territories are impregnated by a sweet and determined sense of Mary in their Christian life. Latin America may be called the continent where daily life is presided over by "Our Lady of Beautiful Love." It is noticeable everywhere, in the mountains, in the valleys, on the coasts, and near the rivers. A great orator has said that the Holy Virgin is American, because she stands so deeply in the hearts of Latin Americans, although they do not always worship her according to the pure definitions of dogma.

From the Catholic point of view, Latin America is the continent where the laity has the most urgent and immediate work to perform.

A famous letter addressed by the Holy See to the Catholic hierarchy of an American country stressed the necessity of a good and opportune solution to serious social problems, in consideration of the great influence this could bear on the future of the Church in this particular country. In an address delivered at the World Congress for the Apostolate of the Laity, Pope Pius XII pointed out some work to be undertaken by laymen, either on the parish or on the university level, which could not be postponed because it concerned as much the defense of the faith as the construction of a world which would not leave any room for the Marxist conception of life. The duty to relieve the clergy from certain matters which can be dealt with competently by the laity becomes ever more serious by reason of the great scarcity of the clergy in Latin America.

In face of an unprecedented increase of the population, in face of a world whose direction has been shifted closer to the middle class, in face of structures which require repair or complete change, in face of so many nations all concerned about their future, the Church has proportionally less clergy at her disposal, and in some countries practically none.

The prayers and the work in favor of sacerdotal vocations is accompanied today by the direction of the laity toward really apostolic works. Otherwise Latin America will be dependent on other continents for the practice of her Catholic life. As with many other truly American things, it will be enough that the seed fall into the furrow to make the crop abundant. The Church of Latin America will one day give back with interest the enormous gift of faith which she received from the missionary people of the sixteenth century.

At the end of a theatrical play, the artists appear again on the scene to identify themselves and receive applause. I too should terminate this modest and brief outline of what we are in Latin America, by introducing to you the great men and women who, during pre-Columbian times and since, have been the leaders, painters, musicians, masters, masons, soldiers, sailors, miners, and shepherds of our great land.

But all the room provided by one of these large pavilions would not be enough to give you a review of all these men, and my voice would not be strong enough to praise the work of the most important among them, illustrious in their mother country for their wisdom, counsel, courage, and audacity. And how could we speak of those who in their hidden way have contributed, maybe even more than the brilliant ones, to the reinforcement of the bases of the Latin-American nations, or who have edified and protected the New World by the sanctity of their lives? Rose of Lima, Francis Solano, Marianita of Jesus, Martin de Porres, the martyrs of the missions, and a thousand others who have been raised on the altars or been forgotten — all are the fruit of American sanctity.

Consider Bolivar, Hidalgo, Sucre, San Martin, Artigas, O'Higgins — there is not a country of Latin America which cannot claim some illustrious father whose features, gestures, and attitudes have become famous and historical.

In the sphere of literature, a summarized history of the writers using the Spanish language would give us more than 1500 illustrious names, without mentioning those who were conspicuous in other arts, such as music, architecture, theater, elocution, painting.

If you want to know them read their books, look at their works, yet reading their names alone would be exhausting. Think of Juana Ines in Mexico and Gabriela Mistral in Chile, Diego de Hojeda, the Inca Garsiloso, the Lisandi and Irrissaris, Bello and Sarmiento, Espejo. By jumping thus from one century to another, from one nation to another, we might perhaps forget Marti, Montalvo, Ruben Dario, Rode, but someone would remember Blest Gana or Hernandez, Vasconcelos or Gallegos, Reyles or Alegria, or Sanchez, and certainly some would not fail to speak about Meruda, de Huidobro, Tristan, Atayde, Mariatgui, Riva Aguéro, Juana, Ibarborou, and Basadre — all these exhibit an extraordinary mixture of styles, disciplines, and ages. But we are not here to make a study of scholars and I am not sufficiently competent to speak about them in their respective order.

To keep silent would be the best way to compliment them, and thus avoid the danger of omitting some illustrious names.

My modest but sincere sketch has given the outlines of history and sometimes perhaps a view to the inside, but my object is also to have a look into the future.

Our view of Latin America would be far more complete if it included some songs and dances by our country people, because the soul of the American people vibrates more in them than in a hundred speeches. It would also be better if we could taste some of the juicy and savory fruits and look at the little flowers, white or red, mauve or blue, gilded and also black.

In the heart of these flowers, fruits, and music we would have the pleasure of showing you the glare of our volcanoes, our waterfalls, our blue and green lakes, the moss of endless shores, the calm of our countries, the greatness of our deserts, the peacefulness of our homesteads, be they poor or rich, but better poor than rich as in a charming song of Caramarque:

> A house here, another a little further,
> and the broad way that comes and goes away.

Yes, the broad way of common destiny that we the American people must learn to follow together.

To follow this way we have common historical origins that unite us from the beginning, and these we might summarize as follows:

History, in its periods of discovery, conquest, colonization, and independence.

Religion, from a common missionary movement, special to this period.

Culture, which is a graft of Spanish culture with native, and the development of which involves mutual influences, as well as a contribution from other Western cultures.

The economy, which, though diversified, offers the common characteristic of a huge potential wealth, so far only partly developed by strong contributions of foreign powers.

The social situation, full of heavy contrasts, especially in a few countries where great intellectual values are mixed with a low average of culture. To this must be added the rapid promotion of the working and middle classes which require sound and rapid orientation.

A political situation which constantly seeks a true democracy, to keep and defend the fundamental liberties of the human person, in countries which still suffer from the effects or defects of dictatorship.

A religious situation with a Catholic base, spotted with Protestantism and submitted to deformations from current official secularism, but obviously demonstrating a rich and entirely Christian spiritual renovation which promises great and vital reforms in all spheres of life.

The Latin American is generous, sentimental, loyal, impulsive, and valiant. He has a love of beauty, music, and justice, is confident and at the same time irresistibly suspicious if he notices that he is cheated. Always hoping in the Providence of each day or in chance, he is also a friend of improvisation and of big but brief efforts. He knows pain and personal joy, his own as well as those of others, and has a strong desire to share them.

And close to these men, poor and rich, is the American woman. Most probably more than man, she gives the tone, color, and depth to the people's soul.

Patient, loving, fruitful, woman is for many men the only thing that remains from Paradise, although she makes them sometimes lose their heads.

Mothers, spouses, brides, we see them in the epic periods of discovery, conquest, colonial organization, and emancipation.

Indian and Spanish and Portuguese women and those of all the people who came to America constitute half of the Latin-American population, and without doubt the better half, especially because women are better keepers of their faith in Christ and their love of Our Lady of Beautiful Love.

Our Lady of Guadalupe, preserve America.

JAPAN

BY DOCTOR JOSEPH SJINJIRO YOKIBE . . . *Born, Japan, 1894; baptized, 1909;* SCHOLASTIC CAREER: *Doctor of Economics (1919); envoy of Japanese Government in Europe (1920–1929); professor, University of Kobe (1929); professor, Imperial University of Kyoto (1938–1940).* DIPLOMATIC CAREER: *to Italy and the Vatican to establish diplomatical relations between the Vatican and Japan (1940); commander of Order of Gregory the Great; commander of Order of San Maurizio e Lazaro.* PUBLICATIONS: Italian Economical Science; About Marxism; The Natural Law According to St. Thomas; History of the Christian Idea of Property; Catholicism in Japan. *This brilliant professor from Japan became sick during his lecture at Brussels. After four months of treatment, he went back to Tokyo where he died after five days.*

It is a great privilege and a pleasure for me to be allowed to address such a distinguished and cultivated audience. I will do my best to open before you the soul of my country and not to conceal its weaknesses and anguish.

This theme has already been treated several times in Japan: for instance, Yoshio Yamada has spoken of the soul of Japan according to classic Japanese authors, and Anezaki has taken the psychological viewpoint and studied the Japanese soul in its three religious and cultural elements: Shintoism, Buddhism, and Confucianism.

This kind of study could be useful for us today, provided we had more leisure. Our Congress is more interested in the psychological analysis of modern humanity. We will therefore present a first element which explains the Japanese soul of today and connects it with its past.

Loyalty and Filial Piety. The spirit of gratitude, loyalty, and filial piety is very much esteemed in Japan. The imperial message, addressed in 1890 by the Emperor Meijy to the Japanese people, says: "Our subjects, with their constant feelings of filial piety, have illustrated its beauty in the course of centuries. Such is the greatness of the fundamental character of our empire; such is also the source of our education."

"Honor thy father and thy mother" is one of the first commandments given by God to men. Jesus said: "Render to Caesar the things that are Caesar's and to God the things that are God's" (Mt. 22:21). And St. Paul said: "Let everyone be subject to the higher authorities, for there exists no authority except from God, and those who exist have been appointed by God. Therefore he who resists the authority resists the ordinance of God; and they that resist bring on themselves condemnation (cf. Rom. 13:1–2). Therefore filial piety and loyalty lie at the bottom of the rights of men and form the second precept of natural law.

God and the Emperor. The dynasty of the imperial family of Japan is one of the best of the whole world. It is the very reason why the imperial Japanese family is more than two thousand years old. Some kings or emperors sought above all to enjoy themselves, but almost none were tyrants. However, when the king and his ministers have no sufficient knowledge of God and the doctrine of Jesus Christ, they may possibly go wrong and think of themselves as God. A persecution may follow, because they consider Christianity as antinational.

The thought of great Japanese minds must also be studied. For instance, Saigô Nanshû, who wrote about the year 1870 and is very much respected for his authority, was not himself a Christian, but he spread ideas connected with Christianity. He said among other things: "Do not deal with man, but deal first with God."

Father Iwashita, who is now considered the most authoritative interpreter of Catholic thought in Japan, and who is also respectfully appreciated in non-Catholic circles in Japan, interpreted the words of Saigô Nanshû in this sense: "The one who can deal with God is really capable of dealing with anyone!" This interpretation of Father Iwashita reminds us of the words of our Lord: "Seek first the kingdom of God and all the rest will be given to you."

These words of Nanshû have pleased me since my childhood:

> Be easy, kindly disposed, but have an iron will!
> Poverty begets the heroic act, and the meritorious act appears in the great difficulties.
> The plum flower opens itself in all its beauty after having endured the snow test.
> The maple's leaves become red after having suffered the first cold of the winter.
> If you truly understand the will of God, you will not seek to live in idleness and lust.

The ideal of Saigô Nanshû was not centered on man or on the king, but on heaven, *Ten*, meaning "God." He was not an egotist, but he had a natural philosophy which respects natural law and natural ethics.

If Catholics could adapt the message of Nanshû and other philosophers and use it to give an interpretation to their supernatural message, they might give a sort of Japanese appearance to Catholicism and make it more attractive for the Japanese masses as well as for the elite. It would thus reach the Japanese soul more quickly and satisfy it more easily. I speak here of the problem of the intellectual adaptation of Catholicism to the Japanese mode of thinking.

I know that the problem is not new. Many missionaries have already written about it. The doctrine of the sovereign pontiffs is very clear on the subject. As far as I am concerned, I was deeply touched by the following words of Pope Pius XII:

> The missionary shall take Charity as a starting point; he shall make his own any truth that the non-Christian has kept in his mind, the good and noble feelings of his heart. He must avoid hurting by being indiscreet; he must keep safe the purity of mind and love of the natives; let him act without jealousy and pride, let him assimilate the wealth of the native culture, and bring them into action after long meditation.

In order to enter more deeply into the study of the rich Japanese culture the Church ought to participate fully in the missionary apostolate. Europe and America already have numerous universities and high institutes. Could it be possible to organize in these establishments a few specialized centers for the study of Indian, Chinese, and Japanese philosophy and spirituality? These three civilizations together include about half the human race, more than twice the total forces of the Catholic Church.

The Japanese Soul: A Mixture of Tradition and Actuality. Since the beginning of Meijian era, when Japan was first opened to foreigners, it has managed to absorb and completely assimilate Western civilization. This was done in record time, and Japan did it without thereby rejecting its own peculiarities. It may therefore be said that Japanese culture today is at the same time oriental and occidental.

However the oriental half is much more intrinsic than the other half of the culture acquired from the West. As evidence of this fact, it is sufficient to spend a few days with a Japanese family and watch the parents and children. A lot of details related to everyday life disclose the bottom of the soul. It is not difficult to notice the difference between the two modes of life, but it is a long way to penetrate successfully inside this soul.

Foreigners who lived a long time in Japan and had opportunity to observe its customs and traditions were amazed to find them yet so pure and varied. It is mostly in the country that it is noticed at best. No doubt, newspapers, illustrated reviews, electricity, and radio are found everywhere, and even television appears more and more. At the present time, there are about a million television sets installed in family homes, boardinghouses, and small inns where people from the neighborhood gather each evening. Notwithstanding the modernity of this device, it brings together a strange mixture of Samurais and cowboys, Geishas and ballerinas, for the enjoyment of people in the most remote spots who appreciate this oriental and occidental mixture.

The soul of Japan has revealed itself to be extremely supple and open in face of the invasion of occidental civilization. It has shown itself to be as described by St. Francis Xavier in his letters: extremely curious to know and to experiment; reflective, sensitive, even sentimental, and at the same time delicate and stoic, concealing its emotions under the appearance of insensibility and betraying them only by delicate and charming gestures.

The epic of a thousand martyrs, during the persecutions of the seventeenth century, showed how the climax of this delicacy was reached, when martyrs wore their best garments, their nicest kimonos, to go to the torture, when they composed a poem at the moment they were fastened to a stake, when they preached and sang hymns from the cross where they suffered agony. It was really a stoical way of being graceful.

This soul appears at its best in the various *ways* or *roads*, sets of training exercises that the Japanese have always liked to practice with an intensity which cannot be found anywhere else in the world. The *Bushi-dô* is the way that leads to the perfect mastery of the warrior: it was the art practiced by the Samurai and by their competitors, the Japanese soldiers of modern wars. If by the overwhelming power of machinery, ancient spirituality has much decreased, there still remain feelings and reactions which proceed from the old military traditions.

The Way of Flowers or *Ikebana* is the art of the house mistress. The harmonious arrangement of a bunch of flowers by a graceful hand can express precise feelings to be conveyed under the circumstances. The neatness of a Japanese sitting room is in strong contrast to the prevailing European taste which clutters the wall and furniture with pictures and all sorts of trinkets. Some of these rooms are almost uninhabitable because of the constant risk of knocking over a vase or a stand. The Japanese does not like this kind of vanity which makes most Europeans happy to display their family souvenirs and wealth. The souvenirs and collections of the Japanese are kept very carefully in the darkness and safety of his *kura* — a little stone house built in the garden. It is fireproof and closed like a safe. Periodically and on the occasion of feasts or visits of distinguished guests, one or two souvenirs or pieces of art will be taken out of the *kura* while some other objects are replaced in their scented wooden boxes. Among other things deposited there, we may mention the painted rolls (*Kakemono*) and family pictures which, together with the bunch of flowers, *Ikebana,* form the main ornament of *Tokonoma* — the attractiveness of the Japanese home.

Then there are the *No* and *Kabuki,* the traditional theater of Japan, and the *Gagaku,* the imperial orchestra which also accompanies ceremonial dances. The refined taste of Japanese audiences is especially revealed by a dramatic play called *No.* Lately, the Rev. Father Hermann Heuvers, parish priest of St. Ignatius at Tokyo, and former rector of the University of Sophia, directed a group of artists acting in the *No* to compose and stage the drama of the Passion and Resurrection of Christ. Through the support and collaboration of the big department stores of Tokyo, splendid brocade costumes and artistic masks were provided for this performance. The drama was played before a most distinguished audience and in compliance with all requirements of Japanese tradition. Being extremely sober, the *No* drama has no actual plot, except the passage or appearance of a personage. The strength of the text and play consists in the use of very sober and limited means to make the expectation of the hero as passionate as possible and his appearance as tragic as possible. The music and the hieratic gestures create a feeling of purification and appeasement, very much appreciated by an initiated audience. To one who remains indifferent to this, or, worse, finds it ridiculous, the way to the Japanese heart and soul will seem long indeed.

I must now say another word about the tea ceremony, which is one of the purest displays of the Japanese soul, and is somewhat connected with the Holy Mass. Among the eight main disciples of the great reformer of the tea ceremony, the famous Bonze Sen Rikkyu, there were five Catholic noblemen. It is said that Sen Rikkyu himself attended Mass several times. His daughter converted to Christianity and died a martyr to purity. Later on, the last missionaries chased out during the great persecution of the seventeenth century were reported to have made some use of this ceremony in order to celebrate the Holy Sacrifice of the Mass in secret. Lastly, during the two centuries of persecutions, certain hidden communities called Sunday "tea day," and took advantage of this tea party to recite their prayers together.

The tea ceremony is a sort of recollection or retreat in which a party of friends gather for a few hours to rest and forget the worries and sorrows of public and business life.

The women wear their kimonos and *obis*, the men their *haoris*; *tabis*, or stockings made of white stuff, cover their feet and they put on wooden *getas* to walk.

After they have washed their fingers for purification at the small fountain in the garden, they cleverly bow down to enter through the tiny door of the tea pavilion. Each one, according to his rank, sits around the room, after having first absorbed himself in contemplation before the almost sacred recess, where the artistic bunch of flowers is placed before the painted roll, *Kakemono*. Everybody kneels on the soft rice straw carpets, the body resting on the heels and the chest erected.

Then the tea master brings the instruments, and in compliance with very strict rites distributes the cakes, pours the green powder and hot water into the cups, mixes them up, and places them in front of the guests. Everything is done silently. Only complimentary remarks are made, and any question must be connected to the ceremony or its instruments, because the persons faithful to this ceremony have a real devotion for its ancient objects and pure matter. Each gesture must be composed very carefully without giving the impression of a command. It consists in the art of performing a rite with a natural and abject bearing. Zen, the spirit of Buddhism, is at the origin of this ceremony which tends to liberate the soul by the concentration of thought and will on simple gestures which must be very distinguished. Liberty of soul and concentration of the attention — this brings us back to the words of Nanshû: "Be easy and very kind." "Do not treat with men, but treat first with God." The liberation of the soul, by the concentration of attention on very simple gestures, prepares the soul for great actions. Interior peace is essential to the planning of heroic acts; whereas dissipation, impatience, and thoughtlessness will finally kill the desire of perfection in a man's heart. *Fascinatio nugacitatis*, fascination with trifles, and *Vanitas Vanitatum* are the great evils that Sen Rikkyu wanted to fight against by his tea ceremony. We must be grateful for it, and it is surely a charming aspect of the Japanese soul. *Virtus in infirmitate perficitur*. A clever use of small means must be considered as very good tactics.

Intellectual Advance by Protestants. The method adopted by the great missionaries for promoting their apostolate in India, China, and Japan is generally well known, namely, the experiments made by famous Fathers like De Nobile, Matteo Ricci, St. Francis Xavier, who addressed themselves first to the elite of the countries where they were sent to preach the Gospel. The successors of St. Francis Xavier, especially Father Alexander Valilagni, made strong efforts to give the evangelical message the utmost dignity and beauty. They introduced printing in Japan and founded colleges and seminaries which had a very high level of studies, probably the highest to be found in all the schools existing in Japan at the time. In their contacts with the leading classes, they brought into action all the arguments they could find to convince them that in becoming Christians they ought not abandon their own culture.

During the modern period and from the beginning of the Meiji period, when the missionaries came back to Japan, they directed their apostolic activity almost exclusively toward the inferior classes. These missionaries came from China, where for several generations the apostolate had to be kept secret. This is the reason why it had not been possible to approach the elite and the formation of the missionaries was deficient: they thought they had been sent first and almost exclusively to teach poor people and merely concerned themselves with spiritual matters. They were rather disdainful of science.

It was rather late in 1888 that the first school for boys appeared, and only two other schools were opened during the next twenty-five years. Tokyo, Osaka, Nagasaki each had a middle school for boys. On account of the lack of teachers and finances, mostly expected from France where a religious crisis occurred at the time, it was not possible to equip and develop these schools properly. They were operated by the Marianist Brothers, pioneers of Catholic education in Japan, who were not prepared for advanced teaching, much less to run a university. On the other hand, the Protestants started immediately with facilities for higher learning, and soon their universities, such as Doshisha, Meiji, Gakuin, Rikkyo Gakuin, Kansei Gakuin, and many others, became very famous. The Protestants may therefore have influenced the composition of the handbooks and history books used in teaching the cultivated milieu. As a result, even the handbooks of the government schools represent Luther as a great hero and genuine reformer of Christianity, whereas the pope is considered as a tyrant.

There are still quite a number of Japanese people who share this disfigured knowledge of Catholicism. They consider it as an oldish form of Christianity, no longer in favor with advanced and modern people who rather believe in Protestantism.

During our stay in Rome, with the members of a Japanese diplomatic mission in Italy, Mr. Ichîzo Kobayashi, a man of outstanding intelligence and former minister in the Konoyé's Cabinet, told me, "Mr. Yokibe, I thought that Catholicism no longer existed in civilized countries of Europe; but here in Italy there are only Catholic churches to be seen, and not a single Protestant church. How is it possible?"

A few French priests tried to fight against this ignorance and prejudice by means of lectures and apologetical pamphlets. I should mention the efforts made by Fathers Ligneul, Vilion, and Drouart de Lezeey. They have cleared the way for a more cultivated and official presentation of Catholic doctrine. Nearer to our time are Father Iwashita and his spiritual pupils, the philosopher Yoshimitsu, the preacher Candau, the jurist and teacher Tanaka Kotaro, and Monsignor J. B. Noda. But it was only the further development which took place after World War II that permitted the publication of an abundant Catholic literature.

Each year the names of new Catholic writers or translators appear in various spheres: catechetics, philosophy, asceticism, mysticism, hagiology, social doctrine. This year, 1958, the translation of the "social Code" composed by the Union of Malines will be published. It is a fundamental work for the study of natural law. This work started in 1913 with the arrival of German Jesuit Fathers in Tokyo, but it will take a further period of almost forty years before it is likely to reach completion.

It is true that during these past years the Catholic Church made a strong effort to relieve this unfortunate situation. Sophia University of the Jesuit Fathers and Seishin University of the Ladies of the Sacred Heart, both in Tokyo, and the Nanzan Institute of the De Steyl Fathers at Nagoya have made great progress. However we have not yet reached the results obtained by the Protestants before World War II.

It may be that we need, first of all, an organization of priests and laymen who could meet regularly to examine the questions of the day, to discuss them and prepare a clear and sound statement, and to have it published by the big newspapers, radio, and television.

Allow me to quote another typical example. Mr. Fukuda (Tokuso), a famous university professor, wrote about forty years ago that all the Fathers of the Church were in favor of Communist doctrine. This statement had not been refuted by any Catholic author. Later, Professor Tatsunosuke Ueda, of the University of Hitotsubashi, who is not a Catholic but is considered a specialist in Thomistic scholasticism, reproached Pope Leo XIII for quoting St. Thomas Aquinas in his encyclical *Rerum Novarum* in order to establish the natural law of private property. But Professor Ueda had only scanty knowledge of natural law as defined by St. Thomas. He thought that it was only the exigencies of nature, in regard to life and reproduction, that could be made an object of natural law. He ignored the fact that, according to the Fathers of the Church, several human rights, such as private property, were considered as natural rights, at least as *praecepta secunda juris naturalis*. Further, Professor Ueda contended that St. Thomas was after all a Communist, because he admitted that, in case of extreme necessity, commodities may be held in common. No doubt, in St. Thomas' opinion, life has a greater value than material goods privately owned, but this does not mean that natural law and private property would be abolished.

These errors, and many others concerning Catholicism, were not refuted during the past forty years. Some remarks may have been uttered within church walls, but the Japanese people and their leaders knew nothing about it.

The Catholic Church, which safeguards the truth, has also the duty to make it known all over the world. In this respect, it must first address itself to the cultured elite of the country. St. Francis Xavier and his successors arrived with letters of introduction from the king of Portugal, the viceroy of India, and the king of Spain. It would be advisable, nowadays, to send Catholic personalities with world-wide reputation to Japan. The recent visit of the French philosopher, Gabriel Marcel, received wide mention in all the non-Catholic press. We sincerely wish that other prominent individuals might help us in our efforts to transmit the true doctrine of Christ.

Recent Progress in the Church. I am told that the progress made in Japan since the end of World War II has been much talked about in Europe. I will summarize that progress in a few figures.

At the end of 1945, the 14 dioceses and apostolic prefectures in Japan had a total of a little over 100,000 Catholics. Half of this number belonged to the diocese of Nagasaki, which had lost more than 8000 Christians by the atomic bomb. The other half were scattered over the four big islands. Honshu, with its big towns, had only 33,000 Catholics. Today there are 250,000 Catholics, which means an increase of 150 per cent. But it is mainly in the long island of Honshu itself that the Christian communities have increased and developed. From 33,000 they went up to 140,000, which is an advance of over 300 per cent.

The forces of the Japanese clergy have increased the same way. After only 18 years the hierarchy is entirely Japanese. But the number of Japanese priests has increased from 150 in 1945 to 350 in 1958 and it will probably reach 1000 in 1970.

The number of Japanese nuns is really extraordinary. There are 3000 nuns who have taken the vows, and 2000 young girls preparing for the religious state in novitiates, probation and teaching houses. This means one vocation for every 25 young Catholic girls.

If these figures cannot convince those who express doubts about the sincerity of Japanese conversions, we can show them the list of our martyrs, which includes some 5000 names and refers to about 100,000 other martyrs.

Moreover, Japanese Catholics interest themselves in the settlements of Japanese emigrants overseas. There are about 200,000 baptized Japanese in South America.

Christian Fidelity. The most striking example of fidelity shown by Japanese hearts is well known to you. The discovery on March 17, 1865, of the hidden Christians is a famous story of the Church, but you probably know nothing of what happened a few weeks ago. A small group of Christians from Urakami, who came on business to Nagasaki, noticed a little building with a cross erected at the top of it in the Port surroundings and located in the new European district. They were rather puzzled and came in, not expecting to find the house occupied by a Protestant parson. They asked to see the church, and were welcomed, but disappointed not to find a single picture of the Holy Virgin carrying the Child Jesus. The parson invited them to come and visit his house and introduced them to his wife. This was a new disappointment, because they realized that these foreigners had not the same heart as theirs. This was not the sort of priest they had been waiting for, for 235 years! They went back to their homes in the small valleys of the mountain to pursue their lives divided between prayer in secret and stimulation from the outside. It was the picture of the Virgin Mary that guided these poor Urakamian peasants to identify the true Church of Christ. The credential they required was the celibacy of the priest.

Later on, when Father Petitjean penetrated for the first time into the villages of Christian fishers of Shittsu, the founders of the community asked him whether he was sent by the Prince of Rome. "The one who will persevere up to the end will be saved."

Influence of Anglo-Saxon Christianity in Japan. The leading classes in Japan were mainly interested in bringing industrial and military power to the country. After 1870 they were convinced that they ought to borrow inspiration and example from Great Britain and the United States. For this reason they chose English as the first foreign language to be taught in the schools and colleges.

The English and North American Protestants took advantage of this fact and became and are still the official teachers of the second official language of the country. The study of English is compulsory in all secondary schools. After the military defeat of France in 1870, the French language disappeared from the official programs.

A great number of youths mustered in force to the Protestant schools, not to receive a religious education, but to learn English and the sciences. No wonder the pupils were influenced by the religion of their teachers. It was the origin of the prejudice felt by the Japanese elite against the so-called "old religion," i.e., Catholicism.

The Catholic missionaries who were mostly French could not read English books, because very often they themselves ignored the language. Recently, on the occasion of the arrival of the Maryknoll Fathers at Kyoto, but also because of frequent contacts since the war with Catholics of the United States, Canada, and Australia, a happy and promising new situation has arisen on this score.

The Church, a Minority. We must not be too sanguine about the progress made so far, because an enormous task remains to be accomplished. A quarter of a million Catholics among more than 92 million means scarcely 1 Catholic for 370 inhabitants. There are still about 50 towns as big as Namur where you cannot find a single priest or Catholic church.

The city of Tokyo, with a larger population than New York, is therefore the biggest in the world. Yet Tokyo contains 35 parishes, each with an average of 1000 Catholics. It is very little in comparison with the number of unbelievers, over a quarter of a million.

The Japanese soul is still free and seeks an ideal. The dream of a world empire, which made the young people so enthusiastic, vanished with the war. This beautiful and generous soul, so much appreciated by St. Francis Xavier, is like a vacant land open to the first occupant. The Catholic Church has all the required qualities to attract this soul. Will it make the necessary effort to reach success?

If we might be allowed to make an appeal to Belgium and to all Europe, let it be as follows:

Send us missionaries in possession of all the treasures of Western Christian culture. We have the right to ask for the sons and daughters of your best families, even those belonging to nobility and royalty.

Send us your renowned Christian scholars, scientists, and artists to act as ambassadors of the truth.

Then equip your missionaries with anything they might need in order to present the message of Christ strongly and clearly.

The Japanese soul is delicate and very fond of beauty and art. The numerous Japanese museums are full of works of art, mainly of Buddhist inspiration, whereas the Catholic churches in Japan are very often built in a faked style, and adorned with plaster statues and bad copies of European pictures.

If a big museum could be erected in Tokyo to contain Christian pictures and sculptures, it would give a tremendous backing to the preaching of the missionaries and be an inducement and source of inspiration to Japanese artists newly converted to Christianity.

The Japanese soul, so anxious to know and love, addresses this fervent appeal to old Europe: You are in possession of all the treasures of the Western Christian culture; do not remain self-satisfied with your wealth of truth and beauty. Do not hesitate to share the best of your youth and material treasures with the Far East.

EUROPE

BY DR. HENDRIK BRUGMANS . . . *Born, Amsterdam, 1906.* EDUCATION: *Amsterdam Lyceum; one year at Paris Lyceum; Doctor (1934), on the thesis* Georges de Porte-Riche, Savie, Son Deuvre; *professor at Terneuzen, Amersfoort, Arnhem, and Amsterdam; president of the Institute for the Emancipation of Workers.* DURING THE WAR: *conceived the idea of "United Europe."* AFTER THE WAR: *Executive Committee of the European Movement; extraordinary professor of Modern French Literature, University of Utrecht (1947); rector of Europe-College at Bruges (1950); joined the Roman Catholic Church (1957); published extensively in Dutch and French languages*

If it is difficult to know oneself and still more difficult to catch the true motives of others, if it is almost impossible to distinguish the mental structures of a collectivity, it would seem to be wrong to attempt to describe the soul of a whole continent which is called a society of societies. There is a strong inducement, either to refuse definitely and simply or to use a limited schematic process, where the spirit of synthesis gets advantage over finesse.

Nevertheless, Europe exists as a community. For all who have visited other continents and come back, there is no doubt that they noticed a peculiar human climate as soon as they crossed the Mediterranean from Port Said to Genoa, or the ocean from New York to Lisbon.

When we speak of Europe, we do not make a synthetic a *priori* judgment. "Typically European" is not equal, in our mind, to "excellent," nor should anything not thought of in Europe be therefore devaluated elsewhere. Europe is not "barbarian," surely, but the land that witnessed the birth and the even temporary triumph of National Socialism can obviously produce perversions worse than the most cruel barbarities. The part of the world that gave the example of nationalism, anti-Jewish campaigning, and a totalitarian spirit should at least have lost a bit of its pride and easy optimism.

On the other hand, I will not load Europe with all the sins of Israel. No use to strike the breast for former generations nor to be shocked by the crimes of the colonists at the moment colonialism expires. I am proud to be a European and have confidence in the future. The whole world is subject to great change, but Europe will turn it into regeneration in the end.

Let us try to paint a "portrait of Europe" (to repeat a title given by my friend and master, Salvador de Madariaga) and do it with an objectiveness that proceeds from true love. Contrary to a common opinion, love is not blind. It permits one to see quite clearly, because there is no need to idealize the object of love artificially. Does not "to love" mean to accept another as he is, without illusions or resentments?

Another introductory remark will bring me *in medias res*. I shall now talk about Europe. No doubt, it cannot be done without reflecting on what happened in former times, but fundamentally it is the present that interests me and the future, because I am more concerned with the younger generation. You will therefore be deceived if you expect a statement dealing with cathedrals and rationalism, crusades and revolutions, or with Joan of Arc and William the Silent.

As a matter of fact, the essential problem for modern Europe is not to remind everyone of her traditions, but to use them as a guide in present circumstances. Europe's treasure is not involved, but a way is sought to use it in a lacerated world becoming gradually inhuman. There is no doubt that Europe has "principles" — their extension is universal — but they are mostly formulated by us in up-to-date terms. How can they be checked by applying them to modern society? That is the question.

It is concerning this question that Europe now interrogates herself and she discovers a bad conscience; she suffers from being off her moral and nervous balance, and she touches near the bottom of nihilism. She believed in so many vain or merely relative values! Must she therefore conclude that everything is fallacious and deceiving? Europe has never felt happy unless she followed her vocation and struggled through her own "heroic and brutal destiny." She notices that what she formerly called her zones of influence are shrinking. She observes that in many places of the world people will forget her rather than be compelled to hate her. And worst of all, she is no longer certain of a destiny to bring a message to the world.

This is especially painful to her, because she can hardly resign herself to living even temporarily in sterility and stagnation. She is not accustomed to it and does not want to adopt such habits. Traditionally she has always been among the leaders of the race around the world. When outrun, she prefers to let the others pass, and keeps aloof and sulky on the edge of the road. She thinks that the concept of progress itself is involved. If others give more efficient directions, it is no doubt because of evil propaganda. Europe, who the day before yesterday seemed to jump over all barriers with ease, is now conscious that human activities have limits, and she finds this tragic.

Is it a simple phenomenon of weariness? By no means only that, for now Europe finds one of her strongest traditions returning. Through her crisis she may yet find her message and even be in advance of her century. For the time being, it is not her contribution to material progress that makes her modern; it is her increasing concern to try to give meaning to this progress. Such a concern must not, however, reduce the speed of the evolution, otherwise all our philosophies would be considered as camouflaged signs of impotency. On the contrary, if the grapes of material progress are not too green for us, nevertheless they often turn out to be "raisins of anger."

Let us pursue this idea. Is it not one of the most durable themes of European history: the dialectic between the impulse of innovation and the wise reflection about relativity? Europe is passionately fond of ascending mountains, in the literal as well as figurative sense. She likes to rush toward new continents. But then suddenly, while in full action, she seems to become giddy and doubtful whether the game is worth the candle. Europe asks herself, why go through all that trouble; is it not a waste of time? After all, would it not be better to confine oneself to contemplation?

At this point, we must remind ourselves that the founder of all European colonization (under all its aspects, one of the biggest achievements of universal history) was at the same time an ascetic calculator, an almost mystical manager, a man of meditation, but willing to take part in crusades. Henry the Navigator could join action to devotion, and this is not exceptional, because the great colonial adventure had always been accompanied by moral and cultural self-criticism. From the time of Montaigne and probably much earlier, since the first Indians gathered by Christopher Columbus landed on European soil, doubts were formulated on all sides concerning our right to colonize. Voices were raised to ask whether modern civilization, as represented by us, is really superior to the one met overseas. At the moment of the most daring European expansion, Europe expresses her doubts. At the time of unscrupulous cruelties, unlimited abuses, the concept of the "good savage" appears, not only in the minds of a few isolated dreamers, but in the depths of the collective soul. At the moment of her most conspicuous material successes, Europe is conscience stricken. Certainly, it is rather seldom noticed by the natives. The fact is nevertheless steadily witnessed in the course of our own history that Europeans are not to be considered merely as dauntless adventurers, efficient settlers, exploiters, and despots who consider the white race as the *Herren Rasse* of the universe.

For anyone who looks a little closer, the picture becomes more complicated and shaded. Beside the conquistador, one finds the skeptic, and sometimes these two contradictory souls abide in the same breast.

Following the progress of centuries, this second voice becomes more and more relevant. The nineteenth century is not only the starting point of the worship rendered to progress, it is also the century of the cultural uneasiness, *das unbehagen in der Kultur,* mentioned by Freud; of the *Welt schmerz,* of the *Spleen,* and of what was called in France *Le Mal du siècle.* With a few and very rare exceptions, such as Kipling, modern imperialism, although a magnificent phenomenon, was never sung by poets. And *Saint Simonisme,* the religion of industrial progress, produced only negligible literary men, poor precursors of the *socialistrealism.*

Thus we conclude at this point that the soul of Europe is twofold. It is the soul of the man of action, who does not stop before any barriers. But it is also the soul of a moralist who contemplates, judges, and makes inquiries.

Nowadays this dialogue extinguishes itself gradually as the standing of the European in the world becomes lower. The tension between the pioneer and the philosopher disappears, because the pioneer no longer has a job. He is turned out of the estates he developed, exploited, terrorized — and loved. He comes back to overcrowded countries where he has nothing to do. Sick of being frustrated, he joins the army of false skeptics. Sick of uneasiness, he becomes an emigrator from the interior. His immense resources, not only technical but human, his energetic potentialities remain unemployed and turn sour. The spleen of the century now affects the group of Europeans who up to this time had cheerfully resisted it.

Therefore, it is unfair to believe that the drama of the lost colonies may be figured in money. For Europe, it is the drama of idleness, the last word being taken in its literal sense: history confiscates the work of those who lived for and by it.

Henceforth, Europe is facing herself alone. She stands before the mirror. She once had a mania to disturb the way of living of all the inhabitants of the earth. She criticized it herself, but she would not get rid of it at any price. Now other people adopt the same mania and get angry with it. This science, for which scientists had worked themselves to death, is consumed everywhere, like an article produced in series.

Today, I dare say, Europe feels as Pythagoras would feel coming back into a class in a modern public college. Someone asks him to explain the law that bears his name, and Pythagoras notices that others have taken his discovery for their own, that he himself ignores some demonstrations of his own theorem, and that any boy will risk more to know about it than he ever did. He feels that people do not appreciate him, that he is ridiculous. When he is turned out of the teacher's room, where as a matter of fact he had been tactless and did not comprehend his young colleagues, he leaves the room very much upset. He rejoins his old fellows, who tell him formally that all mathematics are not by a long way worth a bit of metaphysical truth.

I do not take the defense of my European Pythagoras. I do not say that he is right. I do not state either that the whole of the colonial problem may be summarized so easily. The drawing back of Europe affects us as a spiritual as much as an economic evil, and the European soul suffers by it much more than in its bank account. It would not be enough to give us an "old age pension," supposing the world intended to do so. We must be employed elsewhere, fully employed.

This brings up the question: Is the European materialistic in the daily and commonplace sense of the word?

I am not sure of it. Yet one thing at least is certain: Those who belong to our civilization are tremendously fond of the present life. The great Beyond, proportionately, worries them very little. They were never affected by the problem of metempsychosis. Not a single European philosopher, moralist, or theologian ever considered it a central problem. What counts is the *hic et nunc*, the existence which is actually lived. No one of us thinks that this life on earth is a short episode, a sad moment to go through to other and better lives. The Europeans who are Christians — and they are all Christians, at least according to their ethical concepts — find it normal to be judged by their behavior on this planet. Certainly for the sake of intellectual elegance they may thoughtfully gaze at the skies and remark that no doubt far-off galaxies are thronged with a multitude of races. But, after all, they do not believe it, and the telephone call they expect is much more important than all the Milky Way.

Is this "materialism"? I am not so sure. After all, life on earth was sanctified because God the Son participated in it. Therefore, to consider it as a brief interlude of no importance, preceded and followed by other possible incarnations, seems incompatible with the principle of unique and final Incarnation.

But there is another explanation to our "materialism." It became increasingly difficult for Europeans after the Middle Ages to live an ascetic life. The famous *innerweltliche Askese* of the Calvinist world, this sobriety of daily existence, rests partly on the refusal of dissipation and therefore on considerations of the economic order. But for Europeans, to live well means to indulge in the pleasures of the table. Europe, as well as China, is the mother country of the culinary culture, which was recently expelled from the Anglo-Saxon countries but never totally destroyed. As Li-tai-Po sings of the delicate drunkenness found at the bottom of the jade cups, a modern poet from the Netherlands, and one of the biggest, devotes complete volumes, full of lyricism, to what he calls "his adventures with the table spoon." Elsewhere, he sings lovingly and most cleverly of the fruit of the wine. After all, were the good things on earth created in order that we should abstain from using them? Was it not at the marriage in Cana that Jesus performed His first miracle? These are arguments repeatedly put forward by Europeans, to justify their love of the table.

From the thirteenth century, the *Carmina Burana* sings of the good universal drunkenness. Theology is also concerned with it, and the most clever experts in biblical exegesis bring verses from the Bible in evidence: "Go, eat your bread with joy and drink your wine with a merry heart because God it is now that favors your works" (Eccles. 9:7). But this must not be a bestial comportment. "Happy life" must be organized according to the secrets of an old culture which pays great attention to the kitchen and the cellar. When these disappear, then comes barbarity.

Are Europeans "materialists"? Yes, in proportion to their endeavors to perform, achieve, invest their tremendous capital of energies in profitable undertakings and in accordance with their ignorance of the "gratuitous act." Yes, also, on account of their fondness for good things. But at the back of these two characteristics, the fundamental feature of our soul is to be ever in a hurry.

Because the European does not believe in metempsychosis and

that life on earth is the only one that matters, he knows that life is short, and that *venit mors velociter*. Here the *carpe diem*, the wisdom of the heathen, rejoins Ecclesiastes. There is no time to be lost! Let us work! Enjoy ourselves! We must never lose a minute.

Does it mean that Europeans are upset today by the thought of death? By all means not to the extent that we should be haunted by Dances of Death, as at the end of the Middle Ages. In this sphere, our sensitiveness has become blunt rather than sharper. Nowadays each man of fifty has been through a world war and remembers a preceding one. Moreover, so-called "racial" slaughters were scientifically and methodically organized — another heap of corpses amounting to several millions. Lastly, we know the daily slaughter occasioned by automobile traffic. Death is present everywhere. What can be done? Is it not better not to think about it and hurry along?

Let us hurry, but without taking too many risks! The insecurity of the world makes us prudent, even pusillanimous. When the adventurers are driven back, they become anxious about their old age.

We are facing a strange paradox: the threatened European has become very much concerned about his security; he wants to be covered against all risks. Because anything might happen, one has to set his back up. Because we are exposed to all perils, let us protect ourselves as much as we can.

This is somewhat different from the conquistadores. We find here another very old feature of the traditional human character in Europe. In order to explain the phenomenon, the sociologist would say that the progressive democratization of our society, far from having caused the advent of a revolutionary proletariat, tends to replace the leadership of the gentry by the preponderance of the lower middle class.

And the sociologist would be right, because it seems that everything in Europe has always tended toward middle-class solutions. The roots of our democracy — Middle-Age roots — are to be found in urban, artisan, and, above all, commercial communities. For several centuries, our peasants fought for the rights of private property; this fight was successful in most cases, in the Balkan States, as well as in the Northern countries. Even today, we hear Christian political parties proclaim that private property constitutes one of the main factors of social dignity.

I ought to resist my desire to refer to a valuable judgment, but I cannot do it completely, and I take the opportunity to quote Charles Peguy, when he asserts that the savings-bank pass book ought to be listed on the *index librorum prohibitorum*, because it tends to give a falacious feeling of security by misleading man about his true and fundamental existential misery and the virtue of improvidence.

However it may be, Europe is a middle-class civilization, or she has been ever since the earlier days when she only knew two sides of the picture of ideal humanity: monasticism and chivalry.

The evidence is serious because, unfortunately, the middle class was never a complete leading class; it never presented anything but common-sense rules of conduct, never a true ideal, sage economic expansion, industrial and commercial risk, discipline imposed on oneself to obtain a better crop. Even this meager ideal fades today and an increasing number of voices raise the question: "What will be our fare tomorrow?" They add that the best insured nations have the largest number of suicides and divorces.

Here also we must make ourselves understood. The European soul is not in danger because Europeans eat better than two or three generations ago, or because they are less concerned about material things than they were before. As a rule, insecurity does not foster holiness, although holiness always entails a good deal of inadvertence. On the other hand, the promoters of our security systems were men with an ideal, and therefore inclined to run risks. They reacted violently against a form of society where the masses were handed over to the officials without protection or defense. It is a fact that at the present moment comfort is generally more developed than culture in countries where the social problem is the better solved. A lot of people believe that these countries, more than others, secrete weariness produced by a lack of soul.

Must we tell again why the "supplement of soul" claimed by Bergson will not be infused by a return to the former insecurity? Certainly not. But a real problem remains because the cruel and proud energies let loose during the former days when Europe was governed by the middle class will now vainly seek for an outlet. Without this outlet, sterilized by tediousness, and amid nations lacking vital space, these energies would become nihilist and destructive.

Europe seemed always to fear nothing as much as weariness. The periods of welfare, internal order, peace and good administration are badly appreciated by the historical mythology of Europe. In a middle-class country like France, the adventure keeps all its prestige, and if Louis Philippe, who was the most French of all the French kings, is despised by later generations, Napoleon has his grave at the Invalides, and even the mischievous "Hundred Days" participate in the epic poem.

So Europeans are bourgeois; they become ever more bourgeois, and, further, they have a bad conscience. It seems to me that such is the state of their soul at this very moment, and to such extent that a generalization might be true. Europeans insure themselves against all risks and dream of Apocalypse, with the secret hope of redeeming themselves by doing so.

The individual or collective soul is essentially something anxious. For the Christian who speaks about it, the soul is essentially something to be saved. Anxiety is a sign of life, but of tragic life: S.O.S. — Save Our Souls. What is the use of a soul, if it is not to desire possible salvation? What else but salvation can be offered to it? The soul is not the only vitality of man, although there is no soul without vitality. It does not manifest itself merely by a creative energy that its acts will often contradict. It is the soul that gives true value to all the "good life," as materialistic as it might appear. But the soul does not wear itself out in all this. It is superior, it wants more. It seeks its vocation and destiny. It wants to link itself to other souls in a common aspiration. To revert to the old antithesis of Tönnies between *gesellschaft* and *gemeinschaft:* there is no "community" without a soul, whereas a "society" can survive without it. If Europe wants a community again, she must find her soul again. Such is the meaning of our history in the present phase.

Therefore, nothing seems more absurd than the arguments put

forward by those who pretend to give a new impulse to the European movement by assuring it that through unity our continent will be able to increase its wealth, as if it were wealth that Europe needs! As if it were possible to raise enthusiasm, and to foster a spirit of sacrifice, by giving assurance that the sacrifice is not strictly speaking a real one, because in the long run it will pay! It would be more appropriate to assure the Europeans that they will be able by their union to find new outlets for their needs to launch a tremendous, difficult, and dangerous enterprise. Promises of adventures are welcomed by our civilization which characterizes itself by a terrific need to serve and to act. Wherever the European settles himself, he transforms the surroundings, he destroys, he renovates, very often he corrupts, but he always changes.

The European sticks as much as other people to tradition, but he will change the universe, rather than some of his good or bad habits. In this sphere, let me tell you a true story more eloquent than many statistics. It happened a quarter of a century ago, in a workmen's socialist section. An irritating rivalry opposed the minority left wing to the right wing. The debate went along on every single item of the agenda, even while the Committee, controlled by the right wing, proposed some merely administrative measures, some definite improvements without any political bearing. But the knives were drawn and one had to fight. An argument was put forward by a member of the left wing which should obviously, as it did, disturb the Committee: "But, Mr. Chairman, it is impossible, because we never did it before." The world was about to change its foundations, but to adopt such reform of detail it was necessary to consider whether it had already been done.

Lucky the European who finds the link between the invitation to make a journey and the way back to the sources. He will be followed to the end of the world, beyond all frontiers, provided he keeps faithful to the past.

The Europeans of today are miserable, because they lack at the same time a lively tradition and a future, rootedness and perspective. This is their *mal du Siècle*. Programs and solutions are presented to them. They discuss; and even when they come to an agreement, they are only half convinced. They do not see the ideal; in spite of what they say about it, they feel the need to serve someone. As far as an ideal is concerned, everything seems to require founding and forging again. The continuity is broken, the movement interrupted. Europe is widow of the Ideal. To make herself forget, she tries to act shamelessly, but no role fits her worse, because she remains bourgeois and orthodox in her soul, even in the midst of revolution.

Europe is afraid, but not, as she often says, of the atomic bomb; atomic death is no more horrid than another. "Whoever dies, dies to sorrow," said Villon, and we just had death for our daily companion. No, the real anguish is to find oneself faced with powers that nobody controls any more. In these circumstances, and failing an ideal, Europe takes refuge in the dream, routine, nostalgia. Never have the movies about "the nice period" been more successful. Europe puts on a show of a seemingly indifferent attitude, adopting the policy of an ostrich. "The deluge may come after us." If necessary, she acts according to a sterile agitation which would abolish, for instance, historical facts and declare the atomic bomb "outlaw." So many various forms of "escapism" and fiction. So many attempts to take big vacations and leave modern responsibilities to others — but to whom? So many intoxications, when the feeling of being powerless and afraid is manifested. Europe doubts herself, the world, the future. At bottom, she asks whether life still has a meaning. Youth interrogates the eldest, and these shrug their shoulders. Can these questions be answered? No, they cannot be answered. At the same time, the answer is yes, the answer is readily given: Everything depends upon the angle from which things are considered.

So I believe there is no solution to the fundamental conflict which opposes Communism to any form of Christianity or simply to personalized society. Certainly, I do not believe much in total war, in a press-the-button war. No doubt, nobody will press the button. But we are involved in a religious war, where the borders are nowhere and the fronts anywhere. Whatever she may say or wish, Europe is in the center of the cyclone. Unconsciously she knows it, and that is why she is losing her taste for wine and the culinary art, even for those erotic games so much favored by preceding generations. At the present moment, Maupassant seems to be a very candid author. His pessimism looks rather like a luxury for the well-to-do. Let us repeat it, the danger itself is not the want; it is the uncertainty. For an indefinite period, we are condemned to a war of nerves. On what shall we live during this period? No political remedy gives an answer. But at the basis, everything must be discovered again.

It is precisely this necessity of total discovery that will give us a chance. At the moment when social democratization seems willing to lead toward a universal middle class, the favorite prejudices of any bourgeois life (the certitude for tomorrow) tends to disappear. At the moment we can physically "dress those who are naked," we discover in ourselves a moral nakedness which becomes indecent. At the moment of familial allocations, the very familial principle is challenged by a generation without parents. Now that we have displaced the extreme limits of human power and knowledge, we find the most elementary questions coming to the surface. For the time being, young Europe does not ask a panacea against international tensions. Obscurely she knows that there is none, but she asks for a rule of conduct and behavior. She asks to be heroic, or efficient, or merely honest, but for what, good Lord! And in view of what? When her fundamental attitude shall be fixed, she will also (so she says) solve the problem of Cyprus.

I said it from the beginning, and I repeat it now: the very nature of this statement compels me to make general inferences. Surely I know young people in Europe fight for a solution in Algeria or in the U.N.O., but when I compare the present youth to ourselves at the time between the two wars, a great difference strikes me: the political disengagement. Is it because during these pitiful twenty years between Versailles and Prague we have been saturated with failures? Is it because, for the time being, politics still remain a national thing and the national instrument proves each day its ineffectiveness? We may analyze the reasons, but the fact remains that the most typical representatives of young Europe seem, in my opinion, to aim beyond politics, higher, farther, more deeply.

The hope lies there. And my conclusion follows naturally. How shall I be able to express it, without indulging in the commonplace? Let us be content with a few very simple indications, because Christ will speak while we are silent. Any demonstration would be fruitless, because truth does not spring from discarded error; it is to be found in successful discoveries or in what is rather offered as a favor. They consist less in the acceptance of a dogma, than in the meeting of Someone who lived, was crucified, rose again, and remains present wherever men interrogate Him while they inquire among themselves.

I believe I have a fair knowledge of the European *spleen*. I wonder how to consider it, without speaking about the Lord. It must be talked of very discretely, because anyone who wants nowadays to make himself understood (at least in Europe) must keep extremely reserved. More than ever, we understand why Isaias announced that the Messias "would not raise his voice." But one can talk simply about simple things, without emphasis or false modesty.

At one time, God was taboo in Europe, and it was no more permissible to speak about Him than it was at the time of Queen Victoria to speak in a drawing room about sex. The time has now come when one must get rid of such inhibitions and restrictions. We can no longer afford to discard the essential. At the historical moment we have now reached, there is nothing that stands up straighter in the poor museum of our comforting old things and illusions. Finally we must speak of God.

Europe does not believe any more in her idols, in her "great ideas." In the eighteenth century, she launched the great idea of progress, but she knows now that any progress in any sphere must be paid for by regression elsewhere. She also launched the great ideas of intellectual and civil liberties, but she realizes today that there is no liberty without discipline. She launched the movement of human emancipation, but she notices that emancipation without reintegration amounts to anarchy. She launched the great idea of happiness, and the Constitution of the United States of America postulates that the pursuit of happiness is one of the fundamental rights of man. But there too, Europe now observes, it is not enough to defend men against threatening tyrants; they must also be orientated and directed. One of the greatest prose writers of today, Romain Cary, describes perhaps a whole aspiration, a whole rebellion of the European when he makes one of his characters say: "*Pursuit of happiness.* . . . How dare these people say so! . . . Is sweat and blood, abnegation, devotion, work, and efficiency not enough? How can it be necessary to fight for one's honour, and besides all that defend an honour consisting in being happy. . . . *Pursuit of happiness.* . . . Oh! the pigs!"

Europe no longer believes in her idols, because she has begun to tire of idolatry. It is not that she rejects progress, in order to sink into sterile pessimism. Nor that she does not appreciate the value of intellectual and civic freedoms which are among the stakes of our world fight. Not that she thinks happiness is out of reach and therefore wants to throw herself into the arms of a Moloch who would take little care of individuals and their happiness. The way by which progress can be measured and appreciated must be known in order not to despair of it. An ascetic preparation is necessary to enjoy freedom. To overcome misfortune one must learn to love, which means faithfulness and sacrifice. All these apprenticeships are now going on in the European soul.

Some of our contemporaries imagine they hear everywhere the voice of the demon, shouting: "The stakes are down; nothing goes any more." It is false. But we ought to be saying now: "Nothing goes any more . . . by itself." We live in a period when we must start from nothing and relearn prime truths. This is both an exalting and desperate challenge. It entails a new tendency to accept, invoke, apply to superior authorities. True *leadership* is needed by everyone in Europe, except by those who get drunk on works, fictions, and mediocrity — this last can also intoxicate.

Those who look around and inside themselves wonder whether they are really alone before the mysteries. They are right to wonder, because one cannot discover his rules of living by himself, the same as he is not bound to repeat the adventures of Christopher Columbus on each journey to America.

Discoveries have been made before our time and for our benefit. They are not fatal, but they remain a fact and require examination. Further, they are invested in a big undertaking, which for over nineteen centuries has taken care of souls and is called the Church. Many Europeans, among them the most reluctant, have begun to look it over. They observe that a whole life of exploration is not enough to rediscover the reasons of our worldly effort. They notice also that it is not humiliating to admit that one does not know and that others may perhaps know better. They see that an hierarchical order is not necessarily oppressive, although it may become so, to the individual whose inspiration fails him. They do not rush into the shelter, but they say that, after all, it would be absurd not to go and look at it.

If nothing goes any more by itself, and since it would indeed be stupid to expect to learn everything from personal research, why could not the European soul, cured of its illusions but threatened by chaos, reconcile itself with the Church? The Church indeed bears witness to values and permanent sacred certitudes tested in the course of ages. It professes to serve objectively valid sacraments, whatever might be our transient subjectivity and our psychological dispositions of the moment. It places itself beyond the arbitrary and the contingent. Such arguments do not lead to faith, which is still a gift; but they foster the tendency not to refuse it, if it comes along. A modern Pascal would make it easy to demonstrate that one may or may not believe in the truths of the Church, but these truths correspond exactly to the preoccupations of the human soul and, believed or not, they answer coherently to the inquiries of modern man. True or false, the Church does not offer any outdated considerations.

Sursum Corda! Europeans have transmitted their anxiety to the world, but they willingly run the risk of being the first to be choked by it. They no longer believe so easily that skepticism is a wisdom, uncertainty a liberation, shrugging one's shoulders a proof of intelligence. Certainly they remain inquisitive, indiscreet, difficult to please, anxious to go further into their exploration, always ready to argue whatever is easily and comfortably asserted. God grant that they always remain this way! But doubt is creative only if it gives more light to particular premises and conclusions.

One must endure, adjust, and reach the end. Life is continuity and renewal. Woe to the couples who get caught in the quicksands of routine. Woe also to those, who must start every day from zero to rebuild their love. The *tabula rasa* is not only a symbol of purity, but also of indigence and sterility. It permits one to build. But how is it possible to build while ignoring the laws of construction? The return is to the laws which operate in the European soul.

These are a few reflections upon what I believe to be the present state of Europe, when one tries to penetrate into its subconscious. Great uncertainties are to be found with regard to our future. There is a feeling of bad conscience for the past, mainly for the colonial past; the same amazement that would be felt by a great power finding itself suddenly dethroned. But beyond all these temporal deceptions, we find a real metaphysical anxiety which permits a dream. Not a dream of world power, a restoration of political hegemony, not even a dream of spiritual leadership, which would be pride, but a dream of solidarity and wisdom. We have not only known our own, but we have discovered the illusions of others. We may help the others to be cured. But we should not look at our past with deep regret and consider as the "good old time" the period when our idols still dominated the world. The wisdom of Europe, first continent to be baptized, is not to resemble the weariness with life and skepticism of a badly resigned old man. It is the wisdom of a truly old civilization, but one that is now receiving a treatment of rejuvenation by going back to its sources.

No doubt the practical program for Europe now is union. But the best rational program would be aimless if it were not fostered on the level of personal individual lives. Our greatest temptation of today is anonymity. Our greatest danger is the loss of our spiritual substance. Strangely, we feel the need of meditation, contemplation, devotion, we the sons of the most agitated and active continent. Amid the whistling of the sirens we strongly perceive the sound of the clocks. Are we not called today to pay more attention to them, to make them better heard by the others?

AFRICA

BY FATHER JOSEPH MALULA . . . *Born, Leopoldville, Belgian Congo; educated at Leopoldville and in Bolongo; ordained, Kabua (1946); parish priest, Leopoldville, at Christ the King Parish (1954); traveled through Africa and Europe; noted public speaker*

There are quite a number of works dealing with the black African soul, written by psychologists and philosophers of repute. What could I say further after these erudite and learned books? How can anyone speak of the black soul and make a synthesis of thousands of tribes scattered throughout the great African continent? It is indeed a challenge. Who among you would dare make a synthesis of the white soul of French, Flemish, German, Italian, and Russian people?

But I agreed to make this statement, because I sincerely believe there is something to say about the subject. After several talks with various persons, priests and laymen, exalted and simple people, I will attempt to describe some psychical aspects common to the Bantu soul. I will confine myself, however, to the Bantus living in the Belgian Congo, because I know them best, although some general considerations might also apply to others.

Because of the complexity and extent of the matter, I think it advisable to divide my considerations into three main points: (1) The black soul and the Creator, (2) The black soul and the Gospel, (3) The black soul and the West — political aspirations of the black soul.

1. THE BLACK SOUL AND THE CREATOR

To start with, it is necessary to cancel the equation which some

Western people make between the word "heathen" on the one hand, and the words "savage," "barbarian," and "primitive" on the other. Behind his sometimes rough outward aspect, the heathen hides the noblest feelings of a deep religious mind. In the absence of the knowledge of this religious ground, some Europeans take a silly and sometimes unfair attitude toward the black pagan. It is admitted today that the Bantu knew God long before the arrival of the whites in the African territory. For thousands of years, the Bantu was the *natural man* in the real sense of the word, which means that he lived close to nature and in nature. A rich and exuberant nature announced God; in this nature, the Bantu saw and felt God, and through it he communicated with God. By this permanent contact with the Supreme Being, invisible but visible in nature, the black soul was impregnated and soaked with the idea of God. The Bantu saw the silhouette of the Creator outlined against the surrounding nature. The brutal forces of nature disclosed to him the almightiness of God; the untold wealth at his disposal talked of the infinite goodness of God toward His creatures. God was not far away from His creatures, as it was sometimes alleged; rather, He was close to them. The Bantu lived in an attitude of absolute simplicity, submission, and dependency toward the Supreme Being.

However, this is not specific to the Bantu soul, because men can be seen anywhere who maintain themselves natural, even in civilized countries, namely the peasants who keep their soul deeply religious.

Bangalas call God *Akongo*, the Supreme Being, the Dominator of the universe. By the Bukongo, he is called *Nzambi Pungu*, Almighty God. The Mongos give him the name of *Nzakomba*, the Supreme Being, Creator of everything. By the Balubas He is called *Mvidi Mukulu*, the Ancient One, the First, the One at the origin of all that exists, therefore the Creator, the Eternal. Our African proverbs, taken from nature, are issued from a prodigiously intuitive genius. They condense the whole wisdom of Bantu's soul, and unveil the deep regard of the African for the Supreme Being. When the Muluba worships the Lord and exalts His eminent prerogatives, he will say: "*Maweja mangila, diba katangila tshishiki; wa kutangila diamosha nsense.*" This expression cannot be translated; we try to interpret it by these weak words: "God is the sun that cannot be stared at; the one who dares have a look at it is burned by its rays."

The Bakongo will say: "God has created me with my fingers and my nails," to indicate that everything comes from God, even the things of less importance.

Thus the whole life of the black heathen that is called primitive hides noble religious feelings. From his youth the African learns the word of God from his parents' mouths; he often hears the word of God invoked under various attributes; from his early childhood he is initiated into the religion of his ancestors, mainly in the big circumstances of life, such as circumcision, offering to the manes of the ancestors.

Fetishism. This belief of the black in the Supreme Being has not escaped certain deviations and numerous errors, namely, fetishism, superstition, and magic, so much so that the Bantu seeems to be more concerned with spirits than with the Supreme Being. Therefore, according to the opinion of the whites, the black seems to be enslaved to these things. But how does the black himself regard them? Does he really consider himself as enslaved to all this? I do not think so. For him magic, superstition, fetishism are not slavery, rather they constitute means of protection for his life.

The problem of evil is a universal problem. All men in the world consider life as a great favor. The black only wishes to live and to live better. For him a good life is to have many children and to perpetuate himself in his children; to benefit of the esteem and consideration of his neighbors. He considers a childless home as threatened with malediction. Such a home, sooner or later, will be dislocated, and the husband will be compelled to take another wife to try to have children. According to Bantu mentality, a childless man is a dead and useless man who has not achieved his aim.

The Muluba will continuously address this wish of prosperity to his children: *Kwata ku mundudu,* which means: "Become a man in the full sense of the word, get the utmost vital strength to cultivate the field, go fishing, build huts, and, above all, procreate children."

According to his conception of the world, the Bantu always starts from a principle which is obvious and indisputable for him: God, the Supreme Being, is infinitely good; He is the one who gives life. According to His plan, God does not will evil; He wants man to live, to have children, to reach an old age, and to die as one of God's dead, which means extremely old. He and his children are to enjoy good health and be very prosperous in their enterprises: planting, hunting, fishing, etc.

But when something comes across the way of this divine will, the black mind, with the most natural logicality, begins immediately to look for the reason. The problem of evil springs up in his mind, as in the minds of all men. In the Bantu's mind, the reason is not to be sought in God, who is good by definition; it is therefore to be found in secondary causes, namely, in the harmfulness of creatures, the wickedness of men or bad spirits, which he suspects everywhere. This is the characteristic of all heathen souls, as also of the Bantu's black soul: a propensity to suspect evil everywhere, to interpret every happening in a bad way (the opposite of the Christian spirit); to believe that everything is caused by the wickedness of men or spirits. He will ask himself: "Why suffer? Why cannot my wife give birth to a child? Why is my child dead?" In his mind, the evil is caused and intended by someone. Logically, he will seek means of protection, by making use of something in which, once more according to his conception, God deposited and concealed a force. The intelligence of the simple man, being little concerned with making subtle distinctions between the visible phenomenon and the substratum of this phenomenon, ends by adopting a conception of the world in which the visible and the invisible, natural forces and supranatural, are fatally confused.

Belief in the Survival of the Soul. The black believes in the survival of the soul and in the existence of other kind or mischievous spirits. After death, the soul rejoins the kingdom of ancestors; death does not break the links which unite the living and the dead issued from a common ancestor. The black may have recourse to his ancestors to receive their blessing and their protection against the wickedness of men or the worries of the spirits.

Does not the Church teach us the power of intercession of our brothers who have arrived close to God? Does she not teach us to pray in order that we might one day rejoin them there above? So the Bantu continuously dreams of seeing his parents again, in the great village where there is no more suffering.

However, the access to that kingdom is not available to all the dead. The people reputed bad and wicked, ungodly and dissolute, magicians above all, are inexorably excluded from this village. Their souls wander everywhere in the forests and the plains, in the air and in the waters, until they are reincarnated, born again.

The black lives in this world of invisible spirits; he suspects them everywhere and always. Then he seeks to preserve himself by having recourse to fetishes that heal the sick and assure protection against magic power and bad spirits. But in doing this, he always formulates a restriction: "Provided the All Highest desires it." The Bantu does not consider himself a slave, but fetishes, superstitions, and magic are means, concealed powers, created by God Himself to assure protection and the extension of the life of man upon earth.

These errors are due to the lack of a deep analysis of secondary causes. I want however to stress that these errors are not peculiar to the Bantu soul. In the whole world, wherever faith in God decreases, even in so-called civilized countries, one may notice the appearance of magical practices, superstitions, and fetishes. Chesterton was right when he stated: "When men no longer believe in God, it is not to believe nothing but to believe anything."

It seems to us that Western man has lost sight of the primary cause; he has confined himself to secondary causes. When he wants to reach God, he seeks Him by reasoning; provided he does not lose his way in the maze of his arguments, he will find Him at the end of his syllogism.

Conscious of his technical superiority, exalted by his inventions which astound all humanity, he dreams of nothing but to possess the material world. He forgets that man is only great when he kneels before his Creator. He seems to have broken with God, only to erect another idol: *matter*. We ask ourselves whether Western man has found happiness and peace amid his prodigious technical achievements and his hypercivilized and overcultivated world?

The Bantu, involved in his world of invisible spirits, keeps his inborn sense of God and the correct attitude for all creatures: dependency upon the Supreme Being. The sense of God is one of the African values of which we are proud and jealous; the Westerner may well adopt this value, since he seems to have lost it somewhere.

The Bantu has the right to expect from his civilizers a civilization that respects all his religious tendencies. He rejects as a violent poison all civilization and ideology opposed to his deeply religious aspirations.

2. THE BLACK SOUL AND THE GOSPEL

"Go and teach all nations": this is the formal order given by Christ to His Church. The Church, therefore, received the mission to announce the good news everywhere. Like the leaven in the paste, this good news must penetrate, incarnate all the realities of man, as well as all human institutions, to transform and purify them.

Judging from the results obtained during half a century of evangelization, it must be concluded that the Gospel was enthusiastically accepted by the blacks. In the Belgian Congo and Ruanda Urundi there are 7,000,000 Catholics in a population of 18,000,000 inhabitants. The astounding progress of the propagation of the faith demonstrates that in Africa the seed of the divine word fell on good earth, providentially prepared in advance to receive the message of the Liberator-Christ.

On their arrival in Africa, the missionaries did not find a *tabula rasa*. All the religious aspirations of the black soul were like so many stones waiting to receive the Gospel of Salvation. The purest monotheism everywhere professed by the Bantus offered a solid base on which Catholic doctrine could be constructed. Belief in the survival of the soul and the final reward offered unlimited prospects for expansion. By his clannish conception of the family, his community life, his great hospitality, the Bantu was prepared for universal charity, the quintessence of Christianity.

On their arrival, the missionaries could truly be called the bearers of the Good News that we were waiting for. They could tell us, "The God of your fathers came close to you; he sent His Son, Christ, who made Himself a man to save all men; this Christ calls you now to receive divine life." On the announcement of this Good News, the Bantu soul, with a deep hope for salvation, cheerfully and enthusiastically welcomed the Liberator-Christ and His doctrine.

But Today . . . A new era has opened for the Church of Africa; it comes at the crossing point of a dilemma without middle term. The New Africa that the young Africans seek to build will be either for or against Christ. Who will determine the choice? Africans themselves, of course, because they are free men. But all who have the mission to lead Africa toward its destiny, laymen, missionaries, and members of religious orders, bear a terrible responsibility at this hour. The choice of Africans will depend on the attitude of their leaders and they will accordingly be for or against Christ. In order to save Africa today, the Catholic Church, which Christ wants to be supranational, must raise the standard of Christian charity which does not make distinctions between black and white, poor and rich, and ignores all racial fences, because black and white, rich and poor, are children of the same father: "One baptism, one faith, one Father." This decisive hour requires that the Church and anyone entrusted with the care of souls must give each and all a testimony of genuine charity, without any racial discrimination, and this in order to build a more Christian and brotherly Africa.

What Do We See?

The movements of mass conversion become slower. People are not so enthusiastic as in the beginning. Lassitude is witnessed in the attitude of Christians. The Christianity they bring us now is no longer pure, but a Christianity covered with the cinders of Western materialism. Some black intellectuals show dissatisfaction and even systematic opposition, not toward the Church, but toward missionaries. It is not enough to state the fact; the situation must be diagnosed and the causes determined. I will emphasize only three.

1. Disastrous Confusion Between Church and State. In the beginning of evangelization, Church and State went together. From this close collaboration, an abundant crop issued: the present-day Congo of which we are all proud. But it was a great mistake to create in the mind of the natives a disastrous confusion between Church and State. For them, the Church is the State and the State is the Church. Therefore, they consider religion as a matter concerning the whites: "*Makambo ya mindele wanae*": it is the business of the whites. The two powers are equally charged with colonialism and with perpetuating their paternalism to maintain the black in bondage to the white.

It is time the blacks should go their own way. Further, it is urgent that a genuine Congolese laity be formed, whose duty it will be to incorporate a sincere witnessing to Christ into the new institutions born in the Congo.

2. Materialism and Metropolitan Irreligiousness. Isolation is no longer possible nowadays. The Congo and all Africa are open to all current ideologies: materialism, freemasonry, secret societies, fetishes, and all the superstitions of civilized countries. In the beginning the blacks accepted Christianity as a Western value brought by the whites. Now the same whites bring something else, and the black also accepts it. Formerly one had to be a Christian to be well considered by the white missionaries; now when the African sees white freemasons and liberals, he will become one with them also in order to be well considered. The black accepts all these ideologies with the same calmness and spontaneity as he formerly accepted the Catholic religion. For him, it is "the business of the whites."

3. The Awakening of Black Africa. The slow but steady work of the missionaries in Africa has brought the blacks to a consciousness of themselves. The elite wants to assert its personality and originality. This raises economic and social and even religious problems. The Catholic Church has always appeared to them as the Church of the whites; in African land it has not yet taken on an African physiognomy. The Africans ask themselves whether their religious wealth is not equal to Western values. A few months ago, a black from Leopoldville asked a missionary: "You say that certain rites of the Catholic Church were at the origin heathen rites, but Christianized later on. You came to us in a heathen country. Why have you not proceeded the same way?" This question is oversimplified but it is loaded with dynamite. It states roughly the problem of the necessity of adaptation and reveals the aspiration of the modern African to see the Church take an African physiognomy in African land, to become really catholic, which means the Church of all people.

In the Western Christianity brought to us, it has not always been possible to distinguish what is really divine from what belongs to Western custom. A custom is not Christian merely by virtue of the fact that it is Western. Some Africans wonder whether in the Christianity such as is presented to them it would not be better to cast aside what is merely Western and keep only the divine, what comes from Christ. Extremists go so far as to accept a black Christ, which means a prophet, a Messias of their own race.

We notice nowadays a disturbing prolificness of religious sects and prophets: Neokibangism, Kinduadism, Mpadism, Godonism, Jehovah Witnesses, and other healing prophets. One of these prophets is already preaching racial messianism: Christ is the prophet who was sent to save the whites; Kimbangu is the prophet sent to save the blacks.

Under the circumstances, the adaptation of the evangelical message appears necessary and urgent.

Necessity of Adaptation. The Catholic Church is not Western, Eastern, Northern, or Southern. Its founder, the Saviour Christ, wants it supranational. Thus it must be all this and unite everything in love. Each people must bring its living stone to build the Church.

In Africa, a large part of the population is baptized; Africans have accepted Christianity the same way they have accepted other Western values brought by the whites. Occasionally we may consider some achievements as a miracle of grace; the work of the first hour was superficial everywhere; Christianity is not yet deeply rooted in the souls of individuals; in the mass of our baptized people it may be compared to a veneer.

The work in the depth is about to start now. This work will be performed by the adaptation of the Bantu soul to the message of the Gospel, and to achieve it we need a hierarchy composed of original inhabitants. Knowing better than anyone else the soul of the people and having themselves the same soul, the local clergy only, naturally helped by foreign missionaries, is able to think as Christians with a Bantu mind, and to succeed fully in having this catch hold.

With great effort, the missionaries adapted themselves by studying and talking the language of the natives. Nevertheless, in the eyes of Africans they are and remain foreigners. This is no surprise. Some customs were not completely understood and were stopped by the Western people. The black soul has not been touched yet. The life of the black man presents a duality: on the one hand the Gospel, on the other hand life itself; where compenetration was required, there was merely a superposition; instead of incarnation, it was juxtaposition.

From the liturgical point of view, besides a few sporadic trials, the adaptation is still inactive. With the renovation of the liturgy, we hope the Church doors will be open to worship the Lord with our native songs and our own instruments of music.

Western civilization disturbed the Bantu familial structure which was the foundation of the traditional religion. Individuals became isolated, but the family as such and the customary milieu remained heathen. It has now proved necessary to Christianize the familial African cells.

What do the African families expect from Western civilization? I will tell it in one word: "A deeper love." That's all. Let us first note that Christianization is not Westernization. If Africans agree today to Christianize their families, they absolutely refuse to adopt all Western methods and fashions; they wish to see more love and less individualism. Generally speaking, all those who talk about African families stress first of all the vicious influences of the clan system, which are no doubt real. On the other hand, they talk very highly about the Western family, to such a point that they give the impression that the Christianization of African families would mean the abandoning of the clan system in order to adopt the

Western conception of the family. We know that Western families, besides numerous advantages, give us, by reason of their individualism, an example of a sometimes very poor Christianity which does not fit with our community mentality.

Congolese families, like all the families in the world, have good and bad aspects. Love can be found in married couples and between parents and children. We know very well that this love is far from being perfect. This is the reason it must be purified and sanctified by Christianity.

On the other hand, our clan system presents some definite errors: the desire for lucre shown by the parents makes them bargain in questions of the dowry they claim in compensation for their daughters; these bargainings are sometimes shameful and reduce the personality of the girls; the influence of the parents-in-law and of the grandparents being still strong, the parents do not decide alone and their responsibility is therefore much attenuated. The wife is more attached to her family, to her clan, than to her husband and her homestead — where her treasure is, there will her heart be also. We are certainly fighting these errors and we want to fight them. The natives demand that their Congolese families be respected for everything we can find in them that is good and beautiful: the brotherly solidarity which unites the member of the same family; their great hospitality, their great modesty, and their deep desire to have children. Obviously, the present economic and social circumstances require adaptation. But this does not mean that Congolese families ought merely to be copied from the pattern of European families. This adaptation must be conceived as an incorporation of Christianity into the African homesteads as they are. Genuine Christianity bears in itself the revolutionary ferment capable of transforming our families into homesteads which foster the love and respect of the human person.

3. THE BLACK SOUL AND THE WEST — POLITICAL ASPIRATIONS OF THE BLACK SOUL

While exploring the black soul, we may not keep silent about its political aspirations. Immediately a problem is raised concerning the relations between dominator and dominated, between master and subordinate. Avoiding this problem shows a lack of sincerity and courage, and does nothing toward its solution. Fundamentally the problem is one of human relations, and it will certainly determine a great part of the future relations between Belgium and the Congo. But first of all a few words about the key principles upon which the solution of the human-relations problem rests.

The principle of fundamental equality between races and individuals is admitted everywhere. It is because the whites think that the African is a perfectible man that they undertake the work of civilization and humanization of the Bantu people. All Africans strongly wish that the whites might succeed in their work of humanization by establishing daily and ever more human relations with the natives. The Western people ought to consider the black as a man first, and only thereafter notice the color of his skin. All Africa has only one wish — shared by you in your capacity as Christian humanists and as members of this Congress representing universal Christian humanism — to see the whole world become more brotherly than ever.

The Western has a prejudice against blacks when he lands on African soil: the belief in a fundamental difference between the black and the white man. This is because they talk too much about the black: "The black is this, the black is that, black mentality, black psychology, the philosophy of the black, the intelligence of the black." Some colonials attend lectures or special courses to get a knowledge of the black. God knows what is said in these lectures concerning the black. So the black appears like "a strange beast." This method may present some advantages, but too much talk about the black will create the feeling of fundamental difference. The white becomes the one who invented the wheel, and the black the one who could not invent it. The technical superiority of the Western is indisputable. But there is a risk of creating a pitiful confusion between what makes the objective value of man and the products of his intelligence.

Humanity may not be divided in two: Western and non-Western. There is not a humanity for the civilized and another for the uncivilized. There is only one humanity, which makes all men equal before God and brothers in human nature. The black does not belong to a second-rate humanity or to a humanity participating in Western humanity. Created in the image of God, his soul may be ennobled by divine grace. True humanism is the unfolding of the human into the divine, and the expansion of the divine into the human. Therefore, the black is a man and nothing human is foreign to him. This truth, although theoretically admitted by all, is not put into practice by some who seem to ignore it.

There are no doubt differences between black and white, but these differences are only accidental, due to the influence of the surroundings, heredity, climate, exigencies of life. What is more, these differences may change. We have a good example in the invasion of African territory by Western civilization. The Africans assimilated it, to such an extent that some adopted not merely the Western clothes, but even the Western mentality, the good as well as the bad. Some Congolese are freethinkers. But to a true Congolese a freethinker is a fool. An atheist Congolese is a contradiction in terms. This is the way in which a foreign civilization may transform the mentality of the people they assimiliate, even so far as to dig a trench between two brothers of the same race, a trench that might be as broad as the one separating the white from the black. Although well intentioned, the whites will often stress these accidental differences, and they forget in the end that they are but accidental. It is difficult, in human societies, to understand each other; one is more struck by accidental differences between two human groups, than by their fundamental likenesses. From the moment one believes that the other is "otherwise," it is no longer possible to communicate intimately with him. Philosophy teaches us that differences are the primary cause of opposition, consequently they segregate and keep us at a distance; on the contrary, similitude is the primary cause that brings us together and unites us. The blacks and the whites will understand each other, not by accidental differences, but by their fundamental likeness, i.e., their common human nature. Only then will the white know that in the Congo, like in Belgium, man dances and laughs when cheerful and happy;

he suffers and weeps in pain and sorrow; and the clamor against injustice is neither black nor white, but a human cry.

There is only one way to open the soul of the neighbor; it is to appear like him. The problem of human relations, racial and political conflicts, which divide and oppose men in the Congo, may be solved quietly and peacefully, if we are all conscious of our fundamental equality before God and of our universal brotherhood.

Our accidental differences are such that justice alone is not sufficient to keep our daily human relations harmonious. In order to assure a real union between all who develop the natural resources of the Congo, justice alone is not sufficient; the first thing that shall always and continuously be required is charity and again charity. Without justice, and especially charity, the Belgian-Congolese community is a chimera.

We now witness the awakening of all Africa. The West gave the push that put all Africa on the move. Africa is shaking off a lethargy which lasted several thousand years. Paternalism is saying good-by; colonialism is undergoing a slow but definite death agony. Must we recall the famous words of Mr. Jungers when he was governor general of the Belgian Congo: "The hand stretched forth too late risks being refused"? And these other words pronounced by Governor General Petillon on the occasion of the festival which celebrated the fiftieth anniversary of the Union Minière du Katanga: "The time will come soon when, renouncing the old formula, the black will no longer say to the white, You are my father, but the black will say to the white, You are my brother."

It must be said to the honor of this dying paternalism, that it made the Congo what it is today. But the times have changed. Everywhere in Africa the cry and the aspiration is the same: autonomy. All Africans, standing up and with eyes open, measure the distance which separates them from the big independent nations. Resolutely they will follow the way which will lead them progressively to their internal autonomy. All the merit goes to the West, and the political aspirations of the Africans are to be considered as the normal end of a well-accomplished work.

Everywhere in the world a reasonable desire of emancipation is considered lawful. Why not in the Congo? The Congolese loathe overstrained nationalism. We must, however, note that this nationalism does not come spontaneously. It results from provocations, injustices, claims which were not satisfied, resentments accumulated for years and let loose when paroxysm is reached. In this case it would be a mere replica of European nationalism. You all know the sad consequences of a divided Europe. You endeavor earnestly now to abolish frontiers, to build a scientifically, industrially, and financially united Europe. You are not willing to repeat the sad experiences met in Europe by transplanting in the Congo the fermets of ideologic, linguistic, and racial divisions. The two famous manifestos published in the Belgian Congo, in *Conscience Africaine* and in *Abako,* concerned with the emancipation of the Congo, both publicly and mercilessly condemn the introduction of metropolitan political parties in the Belgian Congo. By giving the example of the unification of Europe, will the West prevent the Congolese from effecting the national unity they aspire to? Some are concerned with the awakening of the Congolese and their claims. They naturally have in mind the events which devastate North Africa. Some even wonder how long the Belgian will remain in the Congo. Why this uneasiness? We have made the Congo together. The Belgians brought their brains, the Congolese offered their arms. But the Congolese are now of age, and they want to speak freely to Belgium in order to determine what exactly their place is in the Congo today. They want to start a conversation to understand each other better, and to reach a better collaboration according to the standards of justice and equality.

What is the object of this conversation? Belgium knows what the Congolese want: It is to collaborate, but in a fair collaboration on a footing of equality, black and whites having the same rights and even chances of access to responsible offices, public as well as private, without racial discrimination on any other limit than the requirements concerning the capacity and competence of each.

The Congolese have been frank toward the government. They now expect the same openness on its part. In their manifesto, published in *Conscience Africaine* in June, 1956, they have clearly expressed their political aspirations: without letting themselves be transformed into European by-products, they will collaborate with Belgium to promote progressively their total emancipation. Their intention is neither to halt nor to make giant steps on the way to autonomy. They ask that the government be frank with them. To leave them waiting and uncertain is taken to mean that Belgium wants to leave them as long as possible in the paternalist regime, even if more or less camouflaged. This is why the Congolese expect that the next legislature will establish a well-defined plan of emancipation. It should grant appeasements concerning the autonomy of the Congo, not by brilliant and declamatory speeches, but by the establishment of a well-defined, step-by-step emancipation plan. The Congolese request that this plan issue not from the brains of the whites only, but that it be the fruit of a sound and healthy collaboration between the whites and blacks. Representative interlocutors ought to be found as soon as possible among the Congolese elite. Consultation with these representatives of the native population and their agreement to work out this emancipation plan will foster the climate of confidence necessary for the achievement of the plan.

Equal Chances. When the Congolese speak about their emancipation, they do not wish that all the whites should leave the Congo. There is a category of whites who are necessary and indispensable to the Congo today. The more intelligent Congolese are very conscious that they need specialists in economic and administrative sciences, medical doctors, engineers, and specialists who take care of them and teach them the secrets of the very complicated machinery which regulates the economy and administration of the country. But we must also admit that another category of whites has proved to be increasingly less necessary in the Congo, and their number ought to be progressively and prudently reduced in the future. In the days to come, consideration shall have to be taken of the truly Congolese elite which is affirmative, anxious to assume responsibility, and rightfully desirous of taking part in the direction of the affairs of the country.

The Congolese elite has truly adopted Western culture and assimilated Western civilization which is fundamentally Christian. Consequently Christianity is the connecting link between Congo and Belgium. To smooth over the jealousies, resentments, quarrels between the races and to safeguard the union between Congo and Belgium, it is necessary to respect the rights of all parties and to extend and intensify Christianity. Congo and Belgium, united by Christianity, will be strong against Islamism and Marxism which constitute the greatest danger to all Africa.

Belgium and Congo are almost compelled to live together; let them try to collaborate fairly, and above all in charity. It is certain that some day the Congo will be independent. It is also certain that in order to reach this independence and to make progress after its acquisition, the Congo will need the help and collaboration of other nations. "To live in a closed vessel is no longer conceivable today" (Dr. Aujoulat).

Better Too Soon Than Too Late. Profiting by the events in other colonies and rich in its own experience, Belgium has all the means at hand to lead the Congo toward its independence quietly and peacefully. Psychologically the whites would like to grant independence a quarter of an hour too late and the blacks would have it a quarter of an hour too soon. Better too soon than too late, if independence can be obtained according to mutual rights and by respecting charity. Coming a little too soon, independence should permit a peaceful coexistence between whites and blacks and a healthy collaboration; coming too late, the solutions might be dictated only by the most unfortunate events and therefore be disastrous.

It is essential that the union between Belgium and the Congo would be freely granted. To this effect the Belgians must keep friendly contacts with the Congolese and deserve their confidence. Is it still possible for Belgium to gain the confidence of the Congolese? Yes, on one condition. That she agree to start the conversation over an emancipation plan elaborated together, and have faith in the possibilities of the Congolese.

We have a beautiful example in the work of evangelization undertaken by the Church in the Congo and Africa. The Catholic

Church gave Africa native priests who are directors of schools, superiors of mission stations, and even bishops. All these have the same full powers and responsibilities as their white colleagues. The work of the Catholic Church in Africa is a success because the Church believed in the possibilities of the Africans. The Congolese expect the same trust from the government. The Congolese elite being very fond of liberty, like other elites all over the world, wants a real participation in the political leadership of its country; it will bear responsibilities for establishing an emancipation plan and be represented in the organizations dealing with the management of the affairs of its country, such as the Colonial Council. The Congolese elite wants responsibility at all levels, not only on the borough level. Why wait any longer to grant responsibility also on the provincial and government plan? Some Africans are capable of learning their job, if they are assisted by experienced advisers.

An economic plan is an excellent thing: erect Inga, provide the country with ways of communications, build hospitals, etc. A human plan is also needed: the *Intelligentia Congolensis* must be at the disposal of the country; capable and conscientious men must be at the service of the masses. They will do it, if they are truly Christians. It is for this reason the Church founded in the Congo the University of Lovanium of which we are proud. It appears necessary, however, to create more scholarship funds to allow deserving and capable Congolese to take higher courses of study in the various spheres of modern technology.

We do not want the work we started together to end up tragically. But the present safeguards the future. For now we must respect everybody's rights and everything specifically peculiar to the African mind; we must have faith in our human brotherhood; we must be just, true, and kind in our human contacts. All men of good will wish that this universal justice and brotherhood may bring peace and harmony between black and white.

THE NEAR EAST

BY ARCHBISHOP PHILIPPE NAVAA (BEYROUTH) . . . *Born, Joun (Lebren), April 18, 1907; student at St. Anne Seminary, Jerusalem; ordained, September 14, 1931; missionary; professor of Theology and Canon Law; superior of the Paulist Seminary; doctor "Summa cum Laude" in the Oriental Church Sciences; consecrated bishop, October 3, 1948*

Something is astir and seething within the Near East. Great conflicts shake these countries and stir up troubles and revolutions. On the banks of the Nile River, as in the deserts of Syria and Arabia, tragic conflicts of interest bring hate and death. Kings are dethroned or drowned in blood. New republics arise. Others disappear to form a great United Arab Republic. The monarchies are disturbed about it and anxious to see all the Arab peoples united, in view of protecting themselves together in a big Federated Arab State.

Amid these serious convulsions of the Near and Middle East, one would like to understand the course of events and the reasons which provoke them. Is it foreign imperialism? Is it hate? Is it ambition for Arabian unity? The truth is that all these causes work together to aggravate the battle which is now fought in the East. But the evil is much deeper and must be found in the soul of the people.

The emancipation of the people of the Near and Middle East is the source of this serious situation. In their hate for the West, which for a long time strongly dominated and enslaved them, these people are anxious to expel the foreigner and fight against the tyranny of colonialism. Now that they are independent and adult, they strive to attain their religious or national aspirations and look themselves to their own glory.

Islam also is awakening and claiming a preponderant role in the Eastern world. One of the dogmas of Islam is the unity of the Moslem community. But how can this unity be effected? And upon what basis? Must the connections with the West be broken? Must unity be founded on religious or moral or linguistic principles? Such are the numerous serious questions which upset the soul of the Near East and require not only temporal arrangement, but truthful, supple, and broad-minded settlement.

Arab Islam, especially, believes that she is called to play a big part in the restoration of Moslem unity. Her direct connections with the Arab Prophet and his country of origin give her full power to speak in the name of the genuine Arabs. Furthermore, the occupation of a central position in the Islamic continent makes it easier for the Arab world to group all Moslem forces and to institute Panarabism.

So the Christian West must be on the watch in order to maintain the best connections with the countries of the Near and Middle East. Otherwise, if the Moslems take a hostile attitude toward the West, the cultural, economic, and political links will be jeopardized and no intercourse will be possible between the Eastern and Western world. It would be so much the more serious if it were no longer possible for the West to show its way to the East, or to help the East find its own way back. But it may possibly not be too late to renew a lasting friendship with people to whom the Christian or de-Christianized West is attached by so many common religious and social interests.

What are the characteristic features of these Near East people? What are the problems set in their souls? What conclusions must be drawn for the establishment of a lasting peace and friendship between the people of the Near East? Such are the great questions I propose. It would be a pleasure for me if the following discussion could give a better knowledge of the soul of the Near East people and make it better loved.

Delimitation of the Subject. At the beginning, a definition is very necessary to delimit the subject and make myself understood.

We must determine the extent of the terms "Near East" and "Middle East."

In the past, the Near East was spoken of only as opposed to the Far East. The Near East included the Western countries of the Mediterranean basin, which belonged to the Hellenic rather than Asiatic civilization. These countries were Turkey, Syria, Lebanon, Palestine, Arabia, Egypt, and Iraq. The Far East included India, China, Japan, and all the people of East Asia.

Recently the Anglo-Saxon people have, for political reasons, adopted the word "Middle East" to designate the countries of the Arab League, and to add certain others, such as Iran, Afghanistan, and even India.

As far as we are concerned, we shall limit our investigations to the people of the Near East properly so called. The subject of our study will be "the soul of the people." Collectivities, like individuals, have indeed a soul. It is through this collective soul that men nurtured by a common religious thought, formed by the same climate, and aspiring to a similar ideal, feel that they are linked one to another in their life and action. By this same common soul people act one upon the other and perpetuate themselves through the ages.

Our inquiry will therefore and above all be a psychological study showing the spiritual values of the people of the Near East and the forces in action to form the modern Near Eastern society.

A general sketch of this society will introduce us to the core of the subject, and will show us the main religious and social problems which disturb the soul of the peoples of the Near East.

The Near East: Community of Moslem Peoples. One seventh of the population of the world is composed of Moslems, the number estimated at 350 million. One quarter of this Moslem population is established in the Near and Middle East. All these Moslems form a huge politico-religious institution which is called the Moslem community, *Al Umma*. Being particular to Islam, this *Umma* is not a union or federation of nations or races politically organized. It is not a religious society like the Christian Church. The community is at the same time religious and political, spiritual and temporal.

It is a true secular theocracy where all the faithful and citizens are united by the same faith and the same sacred Law.

In this community, all the Moslem peoples are united and interdependent. In spite of the borders of the states and differences of origins, the Moslem peoples form, it should be said, only one single people. Islam does not permit any distinction as to nation, race, tribe, or language among its adherents. All Moslem peoples form, therefore, one single community, and all Islam faithful are brothers.

Furthermore, this community of peoples presents itself as universal, perfect, and transcendent. It always urges its members to an ever increasing expansion. The Koran promises the inheritance of the unfaithful nations in a total hegemony "in order that the word of Allah should be the strongest."

This conception of a universal politico-religious community is fundamental in Islam and operates especially in the countries of the Near East. It is at the base of all the religious and social revolutions we witness in the whole Islamic continent and more especially in the Arab countries. It is so deep and so general that it is found in all Moslem souls. It encounters barriers, however, and is limited by some facts pertaining to intermediary communities of tribes and races. The tribes have indeed always caused the Moslems to be divided into wanderers and sedentaries in the same way that race and language have always separated Arabs from non-Arabs. It is above all the national feeling which divides the Moslem community of the Near East into so many different nations, conceived according to a secular and modern manner. Lastly, we have to mention the minority Christian communities which live on Islam soil and cannot be merged into a political and religious Moslem community.

All these tribal, social, and Christian interpenetrations raise for the peoples of the Near East quite a number of serious problems that we should like to study by showing the deep unity of the Moslem community and the not less serious motives which work to divide it.

The unity of the Moslem community is first of a doctrinal order. It is assured by the Koran. This social and religious book fixes for all members of the community and for all the united members the same faith and the same rules of life. All the manifestations of the familial, social, political, and religious life are therefore linked by the same obligations. God Himself interfered to rule this community by dictating the Koran to Mahomet. The Moslem community presents itself as a theocracy, but without clerical organization, with no priesthood, no living magistracy, and no spiritual power in its chiefs. It is a lay theocracy.

The first link uniting the members of this theocratic community is faith in the Koran, considered as a civil and religious code sent by God to unite and guide all faithful Moslems. The very word of God, subsisting in Himself and not created, as the Moslem orthodoxy asserts it, the Koran has been brought to men by Mahomet, who is the last and the seal of the Prophets. Before Mahomet, other prophets like Moses and Jesus taught the word of God. Thus the Moslems, according to the advice of the Koran, must respect the Torah and the Gospel. But anything contained in these two books which is not in accordance with the Koran must be rejected by the Moslems as having been interpolated by the people of the Book or of the Scripture.

A second link of an affective kind unites the members of the Moslem community. It is at the bottom of the heart of every Moslem, and expresses itself on the social plane by common life observances and by a spirit of solidarity and interdependence.

The observances of the common Moslem life are known. They are the prayers said on Fridays, the *zakat* or legal charities, the fasting of the Ramadan, the *hajj* or pilgrimage to the Mecca. These religious or social observances, practiced in common, give the Moslem community its greatest strength of cohesion, action, and vitality. How often in the past history of the large Moslem cities and in the present history of the Arab States, the prayer and the *Khutba* of Friday have been followed by a deep politico-religious disturbance and irresistible popular movement.

From the exodus of the Moslems from Palestine up to the present, Israel is denounced in all the Mosques of the Near East as being the No. 1 enemy of the Arabic States. The revolution in Egypt, the events in Tunisia and Algeria, are commented upon and exaggerated in all the Fridays' *khutbas*, to stir up the people against France and England.

The annual *hajj* of Mecca, which gathers Moslems of all colors and races, provokes similar reactions in the pilgrims and renews each year the exalted celebration of Moslem unity.

The spirit of solidarity and mutual assistance is possibly the deepest feeling of the Moslem community. All the faithful must help each other. A Moslem cannot be the actual exclusive owner of any goods. When a Moslem gives charity, it is not a gift levied on his belongings, but it is God who levies a certain quantity of goods from the share allotted to one to be given to the others. In fact, the help given by the Moslems to their Moslem brothers is very generous. So far the "*Waqfs* goods" have been constituted by such gifts. These goods are given back to God, and the interest accruing therefrom must be spent on pious purposes or public utility works of the Moslem community. Islam is a social institution which limits its scope to the groups united by similar religious links, and in principle it does not reach a human and radiant solidarity.

Finally, the unity of the Moslem community shows itself by solidarity in its claims. This feeling groups all the Moslems against the foreigner and non-Moslem. Today it does not take the form of holy war, but the form of missionary propaganda for the defense of a common good, Islam, or a fight against the colonial powers, against the economical exploitation of the Islam soil, or even against some independent countries risking strong competition against Moslem countries. This propaganda and these claims are in evidence ever more today, here in the national or racial plan, there in the Arab or Islamic plan, always accompanied by great enthusiasm and often successful.

A striking illustration of this spirit of solidarity has just been given by the events in Tunisia and Algeria, by the Egyptian revolution and the creation of the United Arab Republic. If the present master of Egypt has obtained such conspicuous success, if his appeals have been heard in all the Arab countries, if the name of Gamal Abdel-Nasser is mentioned as if he were a hero of Islam, if his portrait adorns all the houses and public places, it is because the

Moslems of all the Arab countries are united and jointly responsible for supporting his claims, and hail him as the chief of Islam and the greatest liberator of the Near East countries since Mahomet and Saladin.

It is this spirit of common life, solidarity, and the repented vindication of it which have always maintained cohesion in the Moslem community. The result is a strong feeling that this is the superior and perfect community which includes, as the Koran says, the best people that ever arose among men (Koran, III, 110).

Therefore it is not surprising that any fault against Moslem unity, any desertion of the *Umma*, any notorious apostasy, any conversion to another religion, should be considered as an unpardonable fault deserving the death penalty. This severity is less the expression of religious fanaticism, as it is conceived today, than the devotion of the Moslems for their community. They imagine it to be the best conceivable state, worthy of the goods of this and the other life. Therefore it is absolutely prohibited for a Moslem to convert from Islamism to another religion and the conversion of Christians to Islam is always encouraged and protected.

Furthermore, Islam imposes on each Moslem the duty of fighting for his community, of defending his faith, by the holy war, the *Gilhad*. This duty, stressed by Mahomet, is also prescribed by Moslem Law, which divides the world in two: "The world of Islam" (*Dar- ul- Islam*) and the "World of the war" (*Dar-ul- harb*). The World of Islam includes the whole of the lands where the Koranic law is followed. Outside these lands, there should be no other than the world of the war.

In its struggle for its faith, Islam tends before all to constitute a universal community and extend its limits to the whole earth. Individual conversions are therefore not of immediate interest for Islam, but they are gladly welcomed. What really matters is the establishment of an enormous community where "the rights of God" will be respected in accordance with the prescriptions of the Koran concerning the religious, social, and political organization of the earthly City. Now these rights will be sufficiently safeguarded, notwithstanding the presence of Christian minorities, in the countries where a local and strong Moslem majority assures the respect of the Koranic laws. The Christian minorities will be tolerated and protected by an institution called the *Dhimma.*

Yet all these conceptions of war and *Dhimma* seem to be overreached today. They mean nothing more than a political claim made by Islam to the world. Islam, as we shall see later, recognizes, in favor of the Christians and the Jews, the right to practice their own religion freely in Moslem countries, provided they shall not disturb Islam and they recognize her superiority.

As for the holy war, for a long time it has been nothing more than a theoretical imperative, no longer directed against Christians. The *Gilhad* has become mere political and religious propaganda for the withdrawal of any foreign domination in Islam territory and for the extension of Islamic religion in the unfaithful countries. The most active center of this missionary propaganda is in the University of Al-Ashar, which sends thousands of missionaries to Africa and to all countries of the Near East.

Of course, these alterations in the Moslem community are not interpreted the same way in the various Arab countries. Will they cause the secularization of Islam and modify its connections with international politics? Will traditional Islam recover itself to form again an enormous Moslem empire? Or shall we assist at the formation of independent Moslem States linked together and with other countries by friendship treaties? The future of Islam will very much depend on social circumstances and on the religious ideal which will be left in her, because in modern Islam there are in fact two souls fighting against each other.

The Struggle of Two Souls. To understand the serious problems which disturb the Islamic world, one ought to revert to the origin of the present renewal movement. Islam dominated the Eastern world up to the sixteenth century. Then she was dominated by the European powers. Today, conscious again of her value, she wants to take back the leading position she occupied before and seeks to renovate all Middle and Near East countries according to the Islamic ideal.

Basically, this general Islamic renewal takes two different directions. The first, given by Puritan reformers, is solely inspired by the religious principles of Islam. The second, given by the secular reformers, would have Islam adapt herself to the conditions of modern society. The Puritans are attached to all the tradition of primitive Islam and want above all a religious reformation and a strengthening of the Moslem community. The secularizers present themselves as modern naturalists and are more or less in favor of a separation between religion and the State. Two souls are opposed in this way and both work for an Islamic renewal.

Arabia was the cradle of the Puritan reformation, whose great promoter was Mohammed ibn Abd-ul-Wahhab. The dynasty of Seouds adopted his reformation and assisted him powerfully. In Egypt, this orthodox reform was launched by Jamal ud-Dine Afghan, and continued by Mouhammad Abduh, the greatest reformer of modern Islam (1849–1905), then by Rachid Rida who died in 1935.

The reformation gave birth to the great organization of the Moslem Brothers (Al-Ikhwan al-Muslimun) whose influence is preponderant today in many countries of the Near East. Over a million Moslems are members of this association, which has a "supreme guide" whom all members must obey. The object of the Moslem Brothers' efforts is the union of all Moslem people into a great Islamic league which must foster peace in the world by preaching the universal principles of Islam. In order to assure this peace and rebuild the former grandeur of the Moslem community, the Moslem Brothers preach the holy war against all enemies, not only against foreigners and "unfaithful" invaders, but also against Moslem "traitors." Two of their watchwords are: "The Koran is our faith" and "The Prophet is our guide."

If Puritan reformers endeavor to renew Islam by re-enforcing all her religious principles, other reformist movements try, on the contrary, to substitute a civil and modern constitution for the religious constitution of Islam. Their main object is to effect the separation of the State from religion, and to imitate Europe in the organization of the modern Moslem States.

This secularizing and modernizing had been initiated by the Moslem intellectuals who were conscious of the internal and external weakness of the Islamic world and who wanted to bring about a renovation by principles of social organization. Masters in Islam, such as the Cheikh Ali Abd-er-Razik and the Cheikh Khalid, have given a philosophical basis for this reformation, stating that the general frames of the social organization of the Moslem community are not revealed, and that Mahomet Prophet must be distinguished from Mahomet Statesman.

The Turkey of Mustapha Kemel Ataturk was the first Moslem country to introduce integral secularity in the organization of the State. This greatest and boldest of all Moslem reforms aroused great sympathy in the Islamic countries. Secularity became an important element in most of the countries of the Middle and Near East without entailing, however, the separation of religion from the State.

So the fight goes on in the soul of the Moslem people, between Puritan and Secularist, between ancient and modern. What will be the issue? The forces are great on both sides. One might think that, after the two big wars of this century, the secularization of Islam was about to be accomplished. Since the last events in Egypt, Islam is back again on the political stage and in the economic world. Far from being diminished, her forces seem to increase and the fight continues desperately in parliaments, newspapers, universities, and even in the street.

The first results of this fight have begun to appear in the constitutions and government rules of the Eastern countries. Integral Islamic Law is in force within three States: Saudi-Arabia, Yemen, and Afghanistan. Eight countries have stated in their constitution that Islam shall be the State religion. Others, like Syria and Turkey, are constitutionally secular States. In the Moslem countries, the State takes either the shape of a theocracy like Yemen, or of a monarchy like Saudi-Arabia, Jordan, Iraq, or of a republic like Egypt, Syria, and Turkey.

In all these countries and systems of government, however, there is an unmistakable Moslem religious predominance. The Moslem Brotherhood of the big community remains a lively reality. Evidence of this fact can be noticed in the United Nations Organization and in the Arab League, where opportunity is often given to the representatives of the Moslem States to assert their Moslem solidarity. It can also be observed in the troubles which arise from time to time in one or another Moslem country and which are reflected immediately in the remotest regions. Islamic hearts in Lebanon, Pakistan, and Indonesia are affected by the sad events taking place in Algeria.

From this quick sketch of the Moslem community, the reader is aware that the religious unity of the Near East people has maintained a general feeling of solidarity among them, but it shows her inability to suppress the racial distinctions and to form independent and lay nations. Furthermore, the withdrawal in 1924 of the Caliphate, which deprived Islam of the Lieutenant of the Prophet, and the emancipation of the civil and penal codes in several Moslem countries, seemed to foster a conception and an achievement of the Moslem society which is increasingly national and secular.

But the principle of narrow nationalism is almost overreached in Europe and in the Near East. And the two new societies, Egypt-Syria and Iraq-Jordan, give an obvious sign that the people of the Near East, far from confining themselves into sovereign and independent States, seek to constitute themselves into powerful federations capable of resisting the big powers of today and of exploiting the extreme wealth of certain areas of their own countries.

The rich oil fields and the determination of the Moslem people to exploit them and to accede again to their former glory might bring together the countries of the Near East in a big political-economic-religious unity and make out of this rich and prosperous Moslem block an essential factor of peace and balance in the world.

Panarabism and Islamic Unity. In the above conception of a sole and universal Moslem community, what becomes of Panarabism, so much talked about today in the countries of the Middle and Near East? Panarabism is a political-religious movement which aims at the unity of the Near East world by creating a community of language and religion. It is a comparatively recent movement, occasioned by the necessity of uniting all parties on a common front to fight the common enemies.

Panarabism introduces into the Moslem communities a new power of integration and unification consisting of the Arabic language and race. The Koran having been dictated in Allah's name, in Arabic and to an Arab Prophet, the Panarabs conclude that the Arab language confers on those who speak it a place of choice in the Moslem community, and that it must unite all those who believe in the Koran.

Panarabism, so conceived, is far from the true conception of the Moslem unity, and it is so much the better understood when one remembers that Islam does not make any distinction of races, nations, tribes, or languages among her adherents. On the contrary, the Koran establishes a perfect equality among all the believers, and calls them all brothers. Louis Gordet, in his beautiful work *La Cité Musulmane*, says rightly: "An exclusive and proud Panarabism is a treason toward Islam; but respect for the Arab race and for a religious unity aiming at social equality is in accordance with the purest tradition" (p. 215).

Islamic Panarabism is also deprived of historical foundations. Truly speaking, the inhabitants of the Arabian Peninsula are the only ones who can properly be called Arabs. The Arab ethnic elements are not so strong in Syria, in Iraq, and far less in Egypt and Lebanon. In any case, Arab does not necessarily mean Moslem. There were and still are, in Jordan, Syria, and Iraq, Arabs who are not Christians and Moslems who are not Arabs. When President Abdel-Nasser says: "The Egyptian people form part of the Arab Nation," he plays upon the words and encroaches on historical truth.

With regard to the part played by the Arabic race and language in the unification and civilization of the Moslem peoples, history shows that it was important but very erratic. At the origin of Islam, a certain superiority was acknowledged to the Arabian race, and the Caliphat of the Omayades was really a great Arabian period, when Islamization went on a par with Arabization, and to such a point that one could not join Islam without being first Arabized.

The end of the National Arab Empire occurred at the beginning of the ninth century with the advent of the Abbasides. Islam became a truly universal religion, and the Islam civilization became richer with many Persian elements. Great Persian statesmen acceded to power and managed the Caliphat in the same way that old Persian kings would have done it. New converts to Islam are welcomed on the same footing as the Moslems belonging to the Arab race, and are not compelled to become Arabic scholars.

From the eleventh to the thirteenth century, the famous dynasties of the Turkish Sultans, Seljuqids and Ayyoubides Kurds, presided over the destinies of Islam. Saladin, the most famous of these Sultans, the one who restored the Moslem unity in the East by throwing down the Fatimite Arab Caliphat of Cairo, and by destroying the Frank kingdom of Palestine and Syria, was himself a Kurd. The Ottoman Turks continued the anti-Arab work of their predecessors, and became, "not without some harm for the Arabic and Moslem culture, the enemies of the Arabs."

At the present time the Panarabic claims are raised again with a new strength. Like Pangermanism and Panslavism, Panarabism presents itself as a doctrine and a political tendency. It aims at Panislamism, at the political union of Islam, based on a tremendous Moslem brotherhood without distinction of race or nation. The Moslem fraternity might replace the racial or regional patriotism in Panarabism. In a speech delivered in parliament, a Moslem from Indonesia said recently that a Moslem from Indonesia was his brother and fellow countryman, more than a Christian from Damas.

In fact, Panarabism endeavors to form several regional groups, with the purpose of uniting the Moslem people into a great Arab nation and a single Mohammedan political block. In 1936, the Eastern pact concluded between four partners, Turkey, Persia, Afghanistan, and Iraq, had little influence over the Arab people. In 1945, the Arabian League appeared with a true Arabic and Mahometan identity. The countries of the Near East adhered to it enthusiastically, encouraged thereto by England, who saw that Islam was an integrating power for all the Eastern countries, affording means to stabilize the Near and Middle East and to safeguard

Britain's interests. But the Arabian League deceived all expectations, the hopes of the West as well as the hopes of the Arabs themselves. In its action, it never reached beyond the stage of discussion and speeches full of vituperation and hate. If the League sank into political nonentity within ten years after its foundation, it was because of the division of the Arab capitals and the irreducible national and racial ambitions which opposed Bagdad, Damas, and Cairo.

Other Panarab unions appear today in the Near East: the United Arab Republic of Egypt and Syria and the Arab Federation of Iraq and Jordan. Will they have better success in grouping the Arab people into one sole Moslem block? The future will tell. But it seems that with the swift evolution of particular nationalisms, the era of the big Islamic empire is henceforth surpassed. Besides, the mystique of Panarabism is negative and deficient. Those who seek to build the Arab nation agree among themselves only to fight and throw out foreigners and non-Arabs. They do not agree to the actual constitution of Panarabism. But, whatever the strength of these attempts at Panarab and Panislamic union, they must not be deprecated because they show Moslem solidarity and the brotherhood of the Believers as lively and stirring realities.

Panislamism and Christianity. Besides Moslem communities, small Christian communities are established in the countries of the Near East. Their existence and merits must be well known in order to properly understand the soul of all the people of these Eastern countries. The Eastern Christian communities are vestiges of the primitive Church which existed long before Islam. How did it happen that Islam occupied their place in Palestine, Syria, Egypt, and Iraq, and dominated them? History explains it fully by the absence of reaction from the Christians who, being tired of the Byzantine domination and hostile to its religious doctrine, preferred to surrender to the Moslem conquerors. This abdication was the gravest and most painful drama of the Christian Near East. By contact with Islam and on account of the very expensive conditions of life which were imposed, the Christian Near East lost her Christianity and became a continent almost exclusively Moslem. Today, in the whole Near East, scarcely four million Christians remain among fifty million Moslems.

How do these few enfeebled Christians live in the great and dominating land of Islam? What is their political, social, and religious condition? What will be their future? These are most important questions which we will have to answer summarily in order to discover the soul of the Christian minority in the Near East.

To be adequate, our answer will consist in making a short historical review, keeping in mind the great difference between the legal condition and the actual condition of the Christian minority living in Islam territory. This distinction, often made in Islam, points up the difference between theory and practice and brings in evidence the social oppression and the unfairness resulting from legal Moslem decrees. The reformers and the legislators of today are willing to abrogate them, but the Moslem tradition opposes an insuperable veto.

In the *Fiqh,* the former law continues to consecrate the supremacy of Islam over all other religions and the social inferiority of Christians in Islam land. It may be that this old law is no longer in force but it is there literally and in its spirit, and it could at any moment be appealed to. It occurs concretely in the relations between the Moslem communities and the Christian communities in the Near East.

Theoretically, the Moslem law is severe and offensive for the Christians living in the land of Islam. Islam, sole sovereign and sacred community, only tolerates and protects the people of the Book or of the Scripture who live on her soil. The Christians may therefore be welcomed on the soil of Islam, but not on equal terms with the Moslems and without any right to amalgamate with them. They may keep their faith and practice their religion, but under certain restrictions and conditions. They are *Dhimmi,* lower-class citizens, who enjoy a protective status called *Dhimma;* but they are compelled to live in a certain state of segregation and humiliation.

The Koran explicitly proclaims this segregation: "O, true believers, do not make friends with those who joked about your religion and considered it as a trifle, nor with those who received the scriptures before you, nor with the unbelievers. But fear Allah, if you are faithful."

This social segregation goes so far that non-Moslems are not entitled to live in the holy towns of Islam, Medina and Mecca, nor to set foot on the soil of their holy places. And in the other Moslem towns, Christians must live and accommodate themselves in quarters separated from those occupied by the Moslems.

The reason for the legal recognition of this inequality is that outside the Moslem community and outside the *Umma* all the others are considered as unbelievers and unfaithful. But the unfaithful have betrayed or at least misrepresented faith in God and refused adherence to the Prophet Mahomet. The Koran blames more especially the Jews for mischievously and deceitfully altering the Scripture, and the Christians for their faith in the incarnation mystery, associating a creature with God (cf. Koran, V, 17 — II; 110–111 — V, 77–79; IV, 51).

It is therefore by reason of their unfaithfulness that they are not equal to the faithful Moslems. This legal inequality is dependent on their religious unfaithfulness. The Christians and the Jews, but the Christians more than the Jews, because they believe in Moses and in Jesus, venerated by the Koran as prophets, will both have citizenship rights in the Moslem community. But these rights will be limited because "these people of the Book" do not believe in the Moslem prophecies. The Koran mentions this fundamental inequality between Moslems and unfaithful. Those, it says, who give associates to God do not keep the sworn faith of a believer, and do not meet their liabilities. These are the transgressors (cf. Koran, IX, 10 — also, II, 79 — V, 15 — IX, 29).

The legal equality refused to the Christians is attenuated, however, in regard to certain points specified in the Koran. The Moslem is allowed to eat the food prepared by the people of the Book, and, therefore, he can have them as servants. He may be married to a Christian or Jewess, but reciprocity is not allowed in this matter (cf. Koran, V, 7). From this it can be seen that Islam assures the people of the Book a real autonomy with regard to their personal status and the organization of their creed. "The people of the Gospel," so tells the Koran, "will judge according to the Gospel" (VI, 46).

However, the people of the Gospel are always requested to rejoin the Moslem community and share its conception of divine unity (cf. Koran, III, 57, 64). Otherwise they are threatened with war and humiliation. "The Christians say that the Messiah is the son of God . . . by saying so, they are like the unfaithful of the old days, and they ought to be punished by God. Make war upon the companions of the men of the Scriptures, who do not profess faith in the truth. Fight them until they pay the tribute . . . and let them be humiliated" (Koran, IX, 30 and 39).

This statute stipulates, for instance, that the Christians will be entitled to keep their churches, but that they will not be allowed to repair them, unless they comply with specified conditions; that they are not entitled to build new churches; that they cannot accept the conversion of a Moslem, but that they must accept the conversion of a Christian. Concerning public offices, Christians are not allowed to exercise functions which would give them jurisdiction over Moslems. In short, the people of the Book who pay tribute to Islam must always take an attitude of inferiority, humiliate themselves, and never expect to be entitled to share the same rights with Moslems.

The reason for this inequality is that, "besides the *Umma*," as stated by Mr. Louis Gordet, "an absolute equality of rights and duty with the believers is not to be thought of (*La Cité Musulmane*, p. 57). Why so? Because according to Moslem law, legal equality is not based upon the natural equality of men, nor upon their common destination to a common social and religious end, but upon their adhesion to the one Moslem faith and their common acceptance of the same rights and obligations.

Islam being by law a politico-religious community, the Moslem alone may have legal equality in this community. The non-Moslems, being outside this sacred community, are unfaithful, or merely tolerated, and cannot obtain the same rights and obligations as the Moslems.

To mark this inequality, the Moslems say that among themselves men are brothers of mud and clay, *Tin,* but that the faithful Moslems are all brothers in religion.

Such is the theoretical regime which rules the Christians in the Land of Islam. Actually this regime was subjected to numerous alterations down through the centuries. It was forbearing under the Omayades Caliphs, it hardened and became malevolent and the persecutor under the Abbassides. With the Ottoman Empire, the status of the protected became an institutional regime. The Christians are constituted in a *Millat,* or nation, presided over by a patriarch. This nation has her particular laws and her own religious tribunals to deal with cases of personal status. But the Christians are kept away from public life.

At present the Christians of the emancipated Near Eastern countries enjoy considerable liberty and equality. They have better access to political life and public offices. They are elected as mayors, judges, deputies; in Syria, Egypt, and Jordan some Christians have become ministers and prime ministers.

This regime of liberty and equality was started by Turkey, who, since 1839, has sought to make the sovereign concessions of the Sultan, available to all the citizens, to whatever religion or sect they might belong (cf. Rondot, *Les Chrétiens d'Orient,* p. 83). Following the example of Turkey, other countries rendered their social laws more supple by no longer permitting a distinction between Moslems and non-Moslems. Moslem and Christian communities are even invited to a perfect equality by the civil laws. One of the most striking examples of present-day spiritual evolution of the people of the Near East is the law related to freedom of thought which was inserted in several Moslem civil codes.

This innovation is a certain sign that further mitigations of the theoretical rights are possible. Those who want this evolution, which is favorable for the Christians, do not fail to quote the Koran itself, when it says the people who are the closest to the Moslems are the Christians, because they have religious and priests.

One must not believe, however, that even in the evolved and modernized Moslem countries, such as Turkey, Egypt, and Syria, the traditional Moslem law has become obsolete. Even if it is no longer sanctioned by contemporary codes, this law continues to exercise its influence on the general mentality of the Moslem people, because they cannot admit that Christians could be entirely equal to the members of the Moslem community.

Difficulties between Moslems and Christians arise from this situation, sometimes in one country, sometimes in another. They do not occur in governmental spheres, nor in the high Moslem society, but in the streets and public places of the smallest villages. There are stories of a great number of troubles created by the common Moslem people against the Christians. Some years ago, some Christians were put to death in Turkey, graves were opened, churches ransacked, priests insulted. The people who committed these sacrileges remained unpunished. Some ghastly scenes took place at Alep in 1955, where assaults were made on the French schools and religious houses. In Lebanon, the publication in 1953 by a Christian called Georges Chacar of a small history book which did not recognize Mahomet's prophetical mission nearly provoked a civil war between Moslems and Christians. In Egypt, the apostasy of the Cophte Church gives evidence of the sufferings she had to endure and foretells a slow and painful death.

At Damas, the *Chari* tribunals take the liberty of overruling the judgments of the Christian tribunals on personal status. To this effect, it is sufficient that one of the Christian parties passes over to Islam and makes an appeal. There was one case of a Catholic Greek husband commanded by the patriarchal tribunal to pay alimony to his wife, but set free from this legal obligation by the Moslem tribunal for the sole reason that the Islam religion he embraced gave him this right against his wife; he remained unfaithful. In another case, it was not only the culprit and apostate husband who was discharged, but the custody of the children was given to him, and they had to follow him in apostasy.

In Egypt, a legal order, given by Abdel-Nasser, suppressed the religious tribunals and prescribed procedures which guarantee to the parties before the civil tribunal that their own law shall be applied to them under condition that they belong to the same faith and rites. But, if one of the parties becomes a Moslem, even during the legal proceedings, the Koranic law shall be applied. So a Christian husband, by converting to the Moslem faith, is entitled to oppose his new rights of repudiation, polygamy, and custody of the children against his wife. This also applies if husband and wife are both Christian, but belong to different communities or rites; they will be judged according to Moslem law.

These cases which are very frequent in some Moslem circles are a very serious problem for the Christian conscience. Can Christians who live in Islamic countries have peace, security, and legal equality with Mohammedans? Or are they condemned to live perpetually in fear, like second-class citizens? And if civil law grants them civil equality with the Moslems, who will bring these laws into force?

If we raise these questions, it is because they vitally concern all Christian souls in the Near East. It must be said that legal equality of Christians is not reached by a mere renewal or readjustment of legal texts, but by a deep reformation of consciences, social manners, and customs.

In short, the Eastern Christians have a right to this legal equality and moral reformation. This right is based on the following reasons:

First, because the Christians of the Near East must not be considered as guests, nor as protected or tolerated people, nor as second-class citizens in their own country. This land belonged to them long before its possession was shared by the Moslems.

Being natives of these countries, they have always lived there, always defended and loved their own country. With a stubborn faithfulness, at the most serious times in history, they kept true to the East, faithful to her traditions, and diffusing her civilization and life everywhere. Today one finds them again on the first rank of the framers of her renaissance, and faithful keepers of her values and independence. The greatest Christian names in Syria, Egypt, and Lebanon mingle now with the greatest Moslem names, in their joint work of modernization of the East and the establishment of Arab nationalism. It is for this first reason that the Christians of the Near East claim a legal equality and expect to realize it fully.

A second reason strengthens their hopes: the evolution of present-day Islam. It gradually approaches constitutional status amid the great Moslem community of independent and sovereign nationalities, where the spiritual is separated from the temporal and where all the citizens, to whatever religion they belong, are ruled by the same civil laws and have in consequence the same rights in, and the same obligations toward, society. This evolution is already an accomplished fact in Turkey, Syria, and Egypt, and everything points to its establishment in all the other countries of the Near East. But Eastern Christianity seeks more than a legal equality. She must liberate herself from certain political and religious concepts of the Moslems, as well as from all material obligations that Islam has imposed upon her. Islam has dominated the countries of the Near East for more than thirteen hundred years. This domination has left marks upon Eastern Christianity which give the impression, not only to Moslems, but also to many Christians, that the Church is a politico-religious institution, that Christianity is also a social ideal, and that the social part is more preponderant than the religious. Rondot says: "The traditional Islam, that could not make a distinction between the profane and the sacred, and therefore considered it a duty to codify society, gave the same direction to Christianity, whose vocation was however essentially spiritual; hence, everything on the social plane induced her to start out as a renovator and even a revolutionary. Eastern Christianity is a long way from complete recovery from this artful deviation, which was much more serious in that it was obtained without real violence" (Rondot, *op. cit.*, p. 91).

Further, the Eastern Church ought to establish a closer and more efficient religious contact with Islam and the countries of the Near East. Growing Islam met on her way a heterodox and disfigured Christianity. The Islam of the twentieth century has no better idea of true Christianity. A meeting of the two big monotheist religions ought to take place. Where could this meeting better be held than in the countries of the Near East? By whom could it be better initiated than by the Christian Arabs or by Arab-speaking people of the East?

To Meet With Islam for a Lasting Friendship. In this general study of the soul of the people of the Near and Middle East, we have outlined the main features of the Moslem community, her religious and social aspiration, her political tendencies, her achievements and misdeeds toward the Eastern Christian communities. In conclusion, we would like to study the means and conditions of a peaceful meeting with Islam in view of a lasting friendship.

So far, the Christian or de-Christianized West has met the Moslem East in order to oppose her. Strong, rich, better equipped intellectually and technically, the West dominated and exploited the people and the wealth of the Near East. Modern Islam has roused up and become conscious of her position and strength. A stream of emancipation has broken through the old dams with a clamor for serious and strong claims.

Islam does not seek a merely political and economic independence of her lands, but claims complete religious and social hegemony for the whole Near and Middle East. What will be the Christian answer to Islam's claims?

To establish a peaceful meeting and a lasting friendship with the Moslems, the Christian answer must be free of all material, political, or economic ambition. It must be entirely spiritual, inspired by the Gospel and matching the Koran in its religious thought. Only meeting with a spiritual purpose will establish Christians and Moslems on a common, solid, and productive ground. In this common work, both Eastern and Western Christians have an important part to play.

The Eastern Christians have been witnesses to Christ in the land of Islam and active collaborators in the renovation of their countries. This double function is essential to their vocation. Witnesses to Christ in the land of Islam, the Eastern Christians have been strong and heroic men, strong as these archipelagoes battered by the waves and never sunk in the bottom of the seas, strong by their faith, by their supernatural courage, by the thousand tricks they had constantly to find out to escape oppression. Sometimes their force has approached heroism, because one needs to be heroic to assure the survival of a Christian people through thirteen centuries of trial and disintegration.

With this same heroism, Islam must be encountered in order to live with her. This meeting is delicate and may even appear dangerous. It must therefore be done under certain conditions and with unmistakable virtue.

First of all, with the strength and courage to avoid the overwhelming difficulties of an Islamo-Christian co-existence.

With prudence and discretion in order not to compromise common interests and to assure continuity of collaboration.

By avoiding any proselytism or public discussion, which on Islam's soil would turn to a disadvantage for Christianity and arouse persecutions and religious wars.

By searching out common points of agreement on both the religious and the political plane.

Religious Islam has many points in common with Christianity: belief in God and a future life. Belief in Providence. Admittance of liberty and merit. Belief in the natural virtues of justice and charity. Condemnation of communism. Mutual assistance and works of social relief. All these doctrines prepare the way for a solid and fruitful collaboration, and may stir up deep and lasting sympathy on the social plane.

On the national plane Islamo-Christian collaboration is so much more efficacious in that it may be effected by unlimited ways and means. Eastern Christians, and, above all those, of recent times, have always been intelligent, active, and faithful agents of this collaboration. They can be found anywhere taking a leading part in the revival of Arabic literature, the emancipation of their countries, the modernization of institutions and codes, and in every initiative to assure social justice, judicial equality, and the conditions required for peace and prosperity.

The equality of Moslems and Christians is a wonderful ideal, and Islamo-Christian co-existence on the soil of Islam is so necessary and urgent that the price must willingly be paid to effect them. This price is twofold:

Christians have been asked to pay the tremendous price of forgetting and forgiving all past humiliations and persecutions. Christians are expected to become a definite part of the State in which they live and work. To put it in one word: unlimited, unfailing friendship is required. Maybe this price, no doubt a big sacrifice, will redeem the faults of the past.

Moslems are requested to pay a just and human price. In order to effect a peaceful and lasting friendship in the Islamic countries, Christians ask that Moslems secularize their civil code and claim true liberty of conscience and true Islamo-Christian equality. This is the price to be paid for the sacrifice asked of Christians and it is the indispensable condition for the safe establishment of peace and concord in the East.

The part to be played by the Christian or de-Christianized West in this Islamo-Christian reconciliation is very important and must be accomplished with much generosity and more unselfishness.

The West has vital connections with the Near East. Since the great colonial expansion of the fourteenth century, Islam has been dominated by foreigners. England, France, Russia, and more recently the United States, seeing that the Near East was a key position, wanted to occupy it in order to open ways for themselves to all parts of the world, and to come into possession of the fabulous wealth of the East. The Eastern oil fields tempt them above all. This oil alone represents half the total oil wealth of the world.

Colonial expansion established only material connections between the West and the East, which deceived Islam. No spiritual contact was established between Christian thought and Moslem thought. Rather, a contact was established in a climate of domination and selfishness which seriously falsified the Christian mystery in the eyes of the Moslems. And in this false perspective, Moslems often think that Islam is far superior to Christianity which installed itself among them through oppression and unjust exploitation.

It is therefore important that the West should completely change her methods of action in the Near East. And as much as it is necessary that the Christian West should be present in the East, let her come with a new spirit. Let her come with the Gospel, the integral Gospel, the Gospel of truth and love, the Gospel of peace and concord, the Gospel of all men and of all times. Let this Gospel not be a dead letter, but an example of life.

In this Gospel, the Moslems find Issa under his true features of prophet and God. And if they do not adore him immediately, they will love him, and his love will do the rest. In the Gospel, the Moslem will find Mary, mother of Jesus. And the mother, so much venerated by the Koran, will lead them to the Jesus of the Gospel.

In this entirely spiritual and evangelical meeting, where they will pray as one, where there will be mutual love, the spirit of God will do the work which seems impossible to men alone. And when the times announced by the prophets arrive, the kings of Arabia will come to recognize the Christ-God and will unite themselves with their Christian brothers in His love.